Games to Play With Babies

Games to Play with Babies

Revised ■ **Expanded**

By Jackie Silberg

Illustrations by Linda Greigg

gryphon house

Mt. Rainier, Maryland

Cover Design: Amanda Wood
Cover Composition: LuAnne Wohler
Cover Photo: © 1993 Elizabeth Hathon

Published by Gryphon House, Inc. 3706 Otis Street,
Mt. Rainier, MD 20712

Library of Congress Cataloging-in-Publication Data

Silberg, Jackie, 1934-
    Games to play with babies / by Jackie Siberg ;   illustrations by
Linda Greigg. —Rev., expanded.
        p. c.m.
    Includes index.
    ISBN 0-87659-162-4 : $12.95
    1. Games. 2. Motor ability in children.   3. Infants.   I. Title.
GV103.S537 1993a   93-17055
790.1'922—dc20   CIP

Table of Contents

Growing and Learning Games

Special Bonding Games

Kitchen Games

Laughing and Having Fun Games

Art and Singing Games

Finger and Toe Games

Bath and Dressing Games

Going to Sleep Games

6—9 months

9—12 months

From the Author

As long as I can remember, I have loved spending time with young children. There is something so joyous in a baby's smile and laughter. For the past fifteen years, I have taught classes for parents and babies together. We share music, movement, games, fun, loving and bonding. The parents have shared with me games that they play with their babies. All the games in this book have been played and enjoyed. They come from a variety of cultures and ethnic backgrounds. They have also been played with "special" children.

In addition to being fun, these games will improve your baby's listening and language skills, curiosity, body awareness and sense of humor. The description of each game explains what your child will learn from playing it.

Games that are played with babies are valuable learning experiences for babies and a bonding experience for both adult and child. Healthy bonding and attachment to a loving caregiver give a baby the emotional security so essential to his or her total development.

Play these games with your baby. Hold your baby close to you and cuddle, pat, touch, kiss and enjoy!!

Jackie Silberg

The age range given for each activity is an approximation. Remember that each child develops at his or her own pace. Use your knowledge of each individual child as the best judgment as to whether an activity is appropriate

Guidelines for Growth

Motor, auditory and visual skills

Holds up his head

Grasps a rattle or a toy

Rolls from back to side

Sits with hand support

Pulls to a sitting position while holding an adult's finger

Follows moving objects with her eyes

Focuses his eyes on small objects

Begins to reach for objects

Picks up blocks

Transfers objects from hand to hand

Reacts with a start to loud noises

Turns her head in the direction of a bell

Turns his head toward the sound of a voice

Responds to a voice with activity

Language and cognitive skills

Babbles and coos

Gurgles upon seeing others

Makes simple sounds like "ahhh" and "oooh"

Says one sound repeatedly

Smiles, giggles and laughs

Attempts to make a variety of sounds

Makes sounds when attended to

Smiles in response to attention

Shows eagerness by making sounds

Fusses when a favorite toy is removed

Responds differently to handling

Reacts to the sight of a toy

Shows awareness of a change in routine

Attempts to repeat motions

Reacts to strangers

Self-concept skills

Inspects her own hands

Brings things to his mouth

Focuses her eyes on her moving hands

Smiles at a mirror image

Makes sounds to mirror images

Anticipates feeding time

Plays unattended for ten minutes or more

Picks up a spoon

Feeds himself crackers

Holds a bottle part of the time

Lifts a cup with a handle

Looks directly at a person's face

Recognizes parents and other familiar people

Reaches for familiar people

Responds to "peek-a-boo"

Smiles in response to facial expressions

Six to Twelve Months

Motor, auditory and visual skills

Bounces up and down in a standing position

Sits unsupported

Pulls pegs from a pegboard

Rolls a ball while sitting

Crawls rapidly

Climbs on stairs

Stands unaided

Moves hand to follow what her eyes focus upon

Picks up small objects with thumb and finger

Puts a few blocks in a cup

Bangs two blocks together

Looks at pictures in a book

Drops small objects into containers

Responds to tones and inflections in voices

Recognizes familiar words and responds accordingly

Shakes a bell in imitation

Stops an activity after hearing "no"

Shows interest in certain words and gestures

Language and cognitive skills

Imitates speech sounds

Babbles rhythmically

Combines two syllables like "Dada" or "Mama"

Imitates the sounds of animals

Says the first real words other than "Mama" and "Dada"

Attracts attention by making noises

Imitates clapping hands

Waves "bye-bye"

Follows simple directions

Understands "no"

Shakes head to indicate "no"

Pulls strings to obtain a toy

Finds a block hidden under a cup

Knows the meaning of "Dada" and "Mama"

Removes a block from a cup when shown

Squeezes toys to make a squeak

Looks to find toys not now in sight

Self-concept skills

Seeks or demands attention

Pushes away another's hands to keep a toy

Holds her arms in front of her face to avoid being washed

Holds his arms out to be picked up

Sucks on soft foods from a spoon

Holds, bites, chews a cracker or a biscuit

Feeds herself with her fingers

Drinks from a cup with help

Controls drooling

Responds to gestures

Plays and enjoys "patty cake"

Repeats a performance when laughed at

Encourages an audience
Cooperates in dressing by holding his arms out

Growing and Learning Games

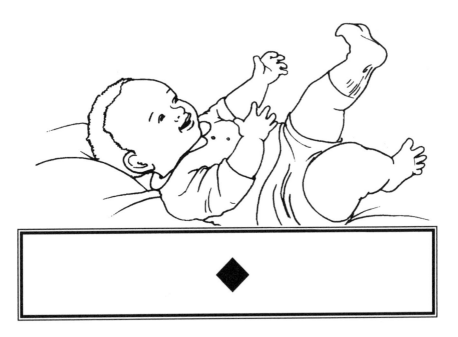

Turn Over, Baby

◆ Babies become aware of their bodies through intentional movements. Turning over by himself or herself is an intentional movement.

◆ Lay the baby on his back. Sit behind his head and hold a small toy above his face.

◆ When you are sure that you have the baby's attention, move the toy over to one side.

◆ Do this very slowly and encourage the baby to grab for the toy. If he turns over, give him the toy to play with.

◆ Repeat the same activity on his other side.

◆ If the baby has part of his body turned and needs a little help, give him a gentle push.

◆ The more you play this game, the sooner the baby will realize that he can turn over by himself, an intentional movement.

WHAT YOUR BABY WILL LEARN:
TO ROLL OVER

Mirror Fun

◆ Put your baby in the crib. The baby's head may be facing forward or to the side.

◆ Place an unbreakable mirror on the side of the crib.

◆ Talk to your baby and, when you are sure she hears your voice, tap your finger on the mirror to get her attention.

◆ The mirror will give the baby something stimulating to do while lying in the crib.

◆ WHAT YOUR BABY WILL LEARN: OBSERVATION SKILLS

Birdie, Birdie, Tweet, Tweet

◆ Hold your baby and look into his eyes.

◆ Slowly wiggle your index finger in front of his eyes to get his attention.

◆ When you have his attention, wiggle your finger to the left and watch his eyes follow it.

◆ Wiggle your finger to the right, and see if he continues to follow with his eyes.

◆ As you wiggle your finger, say:

> *Birdie, birdie, tweet, tweet.*
> *Birdie, birdie, tweet, tweet.*
> *Birdie, birdie, birdie, birdie,*
> *Birdie, birdie, tweet, tweet.*

◆ At the beginning, your baby may only be able to track your finger for a very short period. Keep doing this daily, and you will see progress.

 WHAT YOUR BABY WILL LEARN: OBSERVATION SKILLS

Moving the Picture

◆ Infants are stimulated by vivid colors in a variety of interesting shapes and patterns.

◆ Find a colorful picture of an animal and glue it onto a piece of cardboard.

◆ Punch a hole in the cardboard and thread colorful string through the hole.

◆ Tie the picture securely to the bars of the crib where your baby can see it.

◆ Move the picture to different places in the crib every few days to further stimulate your baby.

◆ Also try moving the picture to other parts of the house.

◆ WHAT YOUR BABY WILL LEARN:
ABOUT SHAPES AND COLORS

Looking at Colors

◆ Visual stimulation is wonderful entertainment for infants.

◆ Gather together colorful scarves and neckties. Twine them around the bars of baby's crib.

◆ Talk to your baby in phrases like, "See the pretty colors," and "Oh, what pretty colors."

◆ Change the baby's position so that she has a variety of colors and patterns to look at.

WHAT YOUR BABY WILL LEARN: ABOUT COLORS

Oh, How Pretty

◆ Babies need visual stimulation. Put a brightly colored sock on the baby's foot.

◆ Move the baby's foot so that he can see the sock.

◆ When he sees the color, he will get very excited.

◆ At first, the baby will see colors accidentally, but he will soon learn to concentrate on a color for a longer time.

◆ Change the sock to the other foot, or put socks on both feet.

◆ Try putting one of the socks on the baby's hand. Watch how he begins to hold his hand in front of his eyes and really concentrate on what he is seeing.

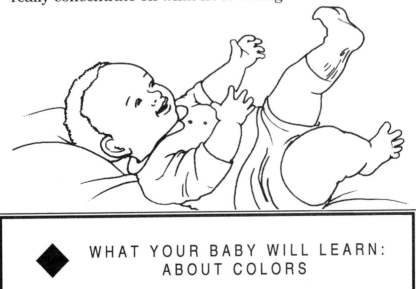

◆ WHAT YOUR BABY WILL LEARN:
ABOUT COLORS

Look, Look, Look

◆ Some research suggests that the more infants are encouraged to look at new objects, the higher they will score on intelligence tests at age four.

◆ Moving your infant to different rooms and to different levels (floor, chair, bed) can make a big difference in what he sees.

◆ Pick three objects. Hold one object in your hand and tell the baby the name of the object. Do the same with the other two objects.

◆ Put each object in your baby's hand, one by one, and say each name again.

◆ The next time you offer the baby the same objects, repeat the game.

◆ A variation of this game is to put the object behind your back and say to the baby, "Where is the _____ ?" Then move the object from behind your back and say, "Here it is."

 WHAT YOUR BABY WILL LEARN:
TO CONCENTRATE

All Around the House

◆ Hold the baby and move about the house talking and demonstrating pairs of opposite actions.

◆ "The light is off...the light is on."

> *"The door is open...the door is closed."*
> *"The towel is on the rack...the towel is on the floor."*
> *"I'm lifting you up...I'm putting you down."*
> *"The cup is full...the cup is empty."*

◆ Performing these actions will motivate the child to do them one day by herself.

 WHAT YOUR BABY WILL LEARN:
ABOUT OPPOSITES

Shake, Shake, Shake

◆ Fill several small plastic containers with different objects like bells, dry beans, rice or marbles. Film canisters and plastic eggs make good containers. **NOTE**: Fasten the lids **securely** so that the baby cannot remove the contents.

◆ Give a container to the baby and, while you are holding the baby's hand, shake the container and say, "shake, shake."

◆ Then give the baby another container and do the same thing.

◆ This is a beginning game that encourages babies to discriminate among sounds which, in turn, promotes language development.

◆ WHAT YOUR BABY WILL LEARN: ABOUT SOUNDS

Kick Those Legs

◆ Put your baby on his back.

◆ Hold his legs at the ankles and bend them at the knee.

◆ Straighten his legs, one at a time, repeating this "kicking" movement several times.

◆ Next bring the two legs together and "kick" them together.

◆ Singing while you do this exercise makes it more fun for the baby. Sing to the tune of "This Old Man."

> *Exercise, exercise,*
> *We are doing exercise.*
> *With a knick knack paddy whack,*
> *Give your dog a bone.*
> *Exercise will make you strong.*

 WHAT YOUR BABY WILL LEARN:
COORDINATION

Talk, Talk, Talk

◆ As babies reach the age of five to six months, before they understand words, they respond to many visual cues.

◆ Talk to your baby, and always tell her what you are going to do before you do it.

◆ Say to her, "I am going to pick you up." Then hold out your arms to offer a visual cue.

◆ Tell the baby things in advance: "I'm going to put you down," "I'm going to change your diaper," "I'm going to give you a kiss."

◆ After you have done this for a while, instead of saying an entire sentence, just say one word: "up," "down," and so forth.

◆ The baby will soon respond to your cues. If you hold out your arms and say the word "up" each time you are going to pick up the baby, she will soon reach out when she sees your arms held out.

WHAT YOUR BABY WILL LEARN:
LANGUAGE SKILLS

Roly-Poly Books

◆ Turn a round container like an oatmeal box into a book for your baby.

◆ Find attractive pictures in magazines to paste them on the box. Select pictures of things that are familiar to your baby, such as animals, people, cups, balls or toys.

◆ Cover the pictures with clear contact paper.

◆ Play with your baby. Roll the box, pointing to the different pictures. Talk about them.

◆ Ask your baby to find a picture: "Where's the doggie?"

 WHAT YOUR BABY WILL LEARN: LANGUAGE SKILLS

Telephone Talk

(This is a wonderful game to develop language)

◆ You will need to get a toy telephone or unplug a real one.

◆ Sit the baby on your lap and hold the phone to your ear as you talk. Say a short sentence: "Hello, _____ (child's name)."

◆ Hold the phone to the baby's ear and repeat the same sentence.

◆ After you have done this a few times, pretend to have a longer conversation of two or three sentences. Use the baby's name in the conversation and other words that he understands like "daddy," "bye-bye," etc.

◆ Next put the phone to the baby's ear, and see whether he will talk into it.

◆ WHAT YOUR BABY WILL LEARN:
LANGUAGE SKILLS

What Toy Is It?

◆ Sit your baby in a high chair.

◆ Pick out three of her favorite toys with one-word names, for example, ball, doll and block.

◆ Pick up the ball and say, "ball."

◆ Pick up the doll and say, "doll."

◆ Do the same with the block.

◆ Ask your baby to pick up the ball. Next ask her to pick up the doll, and then the block.

◆ You many have to do this several times before the baby associates the words with the objects.

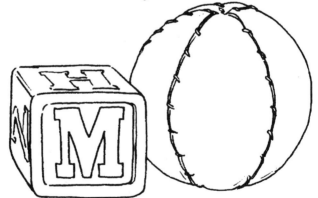

◆ WHAT YOUR BABY WILL LEARN:
LANGUAGE SKILLS

Familiar Sounds

◆ Help make the baby aware of different sounds in his environment.

◆ Each time you want to call attention to a sound, name it for him: telephone, footsteps, running water, doorbell, television, etc. If possible, point to the source of the sound when you naming it.

◆ Take your baby outside and identify the sounds that you hear. Listen for birds, airplanes, children playing, and so on. Again, if you can point to the source of the sound as you name it, this helps focus the baby's attention.

◆ You can also ask the baby a question: "Did you hear the telephone?" Then pick up the telephone and say, "This is the telephone."

 WHAT YOUR BABY WILL LEARN:
LISTENING SKILLS

Fast-Food Fun

◆ Taking a small baby to a fast-food restaurant can be a wonderful learning experience for her, as she encounters new sights and sounds.

◆ You can also make a simple toy to play with in the high chair.

◆ Take the lids from several drinking cups and put them on one straw, leaving space between each lid.

◆ Show the baby how to take the lids off and put them on again.

◆ Let the baby try it by herself.

◆ WHAT YOUR BABY WILL LEARN:
TO MANIPULATE SMALL OBJECTS

Crawling Fun

◆ Set up objects for your baby to crawl over, under and around to help him learn more about the world.

◆ Pile a group of pillows on the floor for him to crawl over.

◆ Put him beside a table that he can crawl under.

◆ Let him chase you around a chair.

◆ Crawl backwards and see whether he can imitate you.

◆ Place a toy on a low chair to encourage him to crawl to the chair and reach for the toy.

WHAT YOUR BABY WILL LEARN:
COORDINATION

Where's the Doll?

◆ When a baby looks at herself in the mirror, she doesn't realize that the image is her own.

◆ Hold your baby's favorite doll or stuffed toy and make it move around. Pretend that the doll is talking.

◆ Now hold the doll in front of a mirror and move it around in the same way. Ask the baby, "Where's the doll?"

◆ Walk away from the mirror. Repeat the activity.

◆ WHAT YOUR BABY WILL LEARN:
OBSERVATION SKILLS

Exploring Game

♦ Find a grassy area with plenty of room for the baby to crawl.

♦ Sit on the grass with the baby in your lap. Pick up a blade of grass and tickle the baby's nose with it, saying, "Grass."

♦ Crawl around in the grass with your baby.

♦ Play hide-and-seek behind a chair or a bush. See whether the baby can find you.

♦ Put some of the baby's favorite toys in the grass. Put them in interesting places so in crawling to them, he explores different surroundings.

♦ Play "wheelbarrow" with your baby. Lift his legs off the ground and let him crawl with his hands.

 WHAT YOUR BABY WILL LEARN:
EXPLORATION SKILLS

Texture Crawl

◆ Find articles that have interesting textures, such as a rubber floor mat, throw rug, carpet samples, soft blanket, silk scarf or velvet scrap.

◆ Lay the articles on the floor and crawl with the baby over them, one at a time.

◆ As you crawl, describe the texture with words like smooth, bumpy, cool, etc.

◆ When you have done this many times, rearrange the articles in a different order.

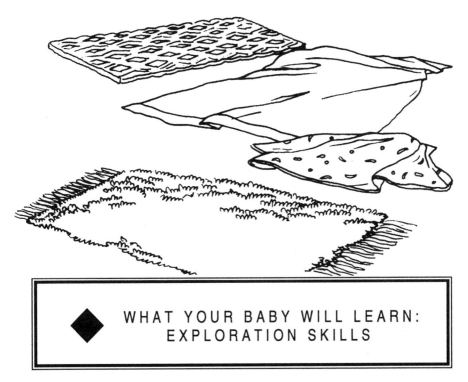

◆ WHAT YOUR BABY WILL LEARN:
EXPLORATION SKILLS

Look, I Can Pour!

◆ Sit on the floor with your baby. Place paper cups filled with dry cereal in front of you. Round oat cereals work well.

◆ Show the baby how to pour the cereal from one cup to another. Then let the baby try to pour.

◆ Little ones will spend a lot of time doing this activity until they get it right. They also enjoy eating what spills.

◆ The next step in learning how to pour is to work with water. That will come much later.

◆ WHAT YOUR BABY WILL LEARN:
COORDINATION

Boxes, Boxes

◆ There are many ways to use boxes to help your baby develop her ability to use her hands.

◆ Find boxes with tops. Show the baby how to take the top off a box and then put it back on. Vary the sizes and textures of the boxes.

◆ Boxes make great receptacles for toys, blocks and clothespins. Show the baby how to drop things into a box and then turn it over to retrieve them. **NOTE**: Only use objects that are too large for the baby to swallow.

◆ Boxes are also fun as make-believe telephones, hats and megaphones.

◆ Hold a box in front of your mouth and talk into it. Say your baby's name.

 **WHAT YOUR BABY WILL LEARN:
COORDINATION**

Drop the Clothespin

◆ The object of this game is to drop clothespins into a container.

◆ You can use an empty coffee can or cut a large opening in an empty gallon milk container. **NOTE**: Be sure the coffee can has no rough edges.

◆ Show the baby how to hold the clothespin to drop it into the opening. If you tilt the container at first, it will help the baby succeed.

◆ Show the baby how to turn the container upside down to remove the clothespins.

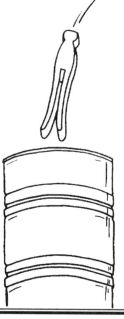

◆ WHAT YOUR BABY WILL LEARN:
FUN

MONTHS

Roll It Back

◆ You will need a soft fabric ball.

◆ Sit on the floor facing your baby and roll the ball towards him.

◆ Take the baby's hands and show him how to roll the ball back to you.

◆ This is great fun for the baby and, with a little encouragement, he will learn very quickly to roll the ball back.

◆ Once babies start throwing things out of the crib, it is a sign that they are ready to play this game.

 WHAT YOUR BABY WILL LEARN: TO ROLL A BALL

9-12
MONTHS

Ribbon Fun

◆ Pick three of your baby's favorite toys and tie a ribbon around each.

◆ Show the baby how to pull the ribbon to get the toy.

◆ Ask her to give you a toy. Put her hand on the ribbon that she needs to pull. You may have to help her at first.

◆ After a few tries, she will be able to pull the toy without any problem.

◆ Ask her to give you each toy tied with a ribbon.

◆ Try hiding a toy with just the ribbon showing. Ask the baby where the toy is and show her how to pull the ribbon to get the toy.

◆ She will love doing this and laugh with great enthusiasm.

◆ WHAT YOUR BABY WILL LEARN:
TO FOLLOW DIRECTIONS

Doll Games

◆ Sit your baby in your lap. Stroke her hair and say, "Pretty hair."

◆ Put the baby's hands on your hair and say, "Daddy's hair."

◆ Run a comb through your baby's hair.

◆ Show your baby how you comb your hair.

◆ Find a doll with hair and run the comb through its hair.

◆ Give the doll to your baby and ask her to comb the doll's hair.

◆ Ask the baby to comb her own hair.

◆ Ask the baby to comb your hair.

 WHAT YOUR BABY WILL LEARN:
TO FOLLOW DIRECTIONS

Where's the Foot?

◆ Draw a picture of a baby on a large piece of heavy paper.

◆ Glue pieces of material over individual part of the body like hands, head, toes, knees and tummy.

◆ Ask your baby, "Where's the baby's head?" Lift up the material covering the head and say, "Hello, head!"

◆ Continue this game, naming the other parts.

◆ Soon your baby will be playing this game by himself.

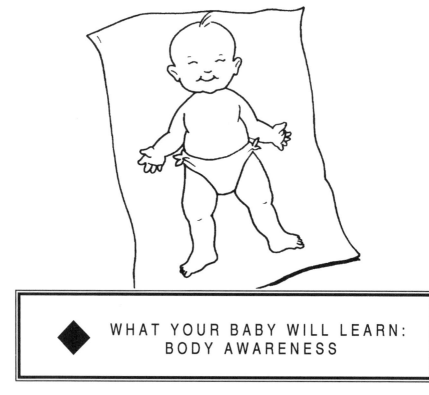

◆ WHAT YOUR BABY WILL LEARN:
BODY AWARENESS

Left, Right, Cross the Street

◆ When crossing the street with your baby, play this game.

◆ Say to the baby, "Now we are at the corner. We are going to cross the street. Let's make sure no cars are coming. Look to the left." Turn the stroller or the child to the left.

◆ Now say, "No cars. Okay, now let's look to the right." Turn the stroller or the child to the right.

◆ Next say, "No cars. Good. It's okay to cross the street."

◆ The child is learning traffic safety and the concept of left and right.

WHAT YOUR BABY WILL LEARN:
SAFETY SKILLS

Gathering Treasures

◆ The outdoors is a wonderful place for exploring and discovering.

◆ Take a bucket outside and help your baby discover rocks, leaves, branches and twigs into it.

◆ Bring the bucket to a comfortable place and dump everything out.

◆ Let her hold the rocks, the leaves, and so on in her hand while you tell her the name of each treasure.

◆ Your baby will enjoy putting the treasures back into the bucket and dumping them out again.

◆ Ask her to give you a leaf or a rock.

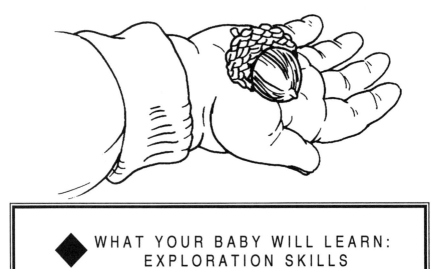

◆ WHAT YOUR BABY WILL LEARN:
EXPLORATION SKILLS

Where Did It Go?

◆ This game helps your baby learn that an object still exists even if it's out of sight.

◆ Sit on the floor with your baby and show him a favorite toy.

◆ Let the baby play with the toy for a few minutes, then ask him if you may have a turn.

◆ If he agrees, take the toy and cover it with a cloth easily within the baby's reach.

◆ Help him to find the toy, then repeat the game. Ask him, "Where is the toy?" or something similar. Make a mystery out of the game.

◆ Play the game several times until the baby understands where the toy is and retrieves it.

◆ Repeat the game with a different toy or object.

 WHAT YOUR BABY WILL LEARN:
COGNITIVE SKILLS

Now It's Three

♦ Sit on the floor with your baby facing you.

♦ Give the baby a small toy to hold in her hand.

♦ Once she has a good grasp on the toy, give her a second toy to hold in her other hand.

♦ Once she is able to hold a toy in each hand, offer her a third toy. At first, she will try to grasp the toy with a full hand, but soon she will figure out how to put one toy down in order to pick another toy up.

◆ WHAT YOUR BABY WILL LEARN:
PROBLEM-SOLVING SKILLS

Pushing Game

◆ When your baby first learns to walk, he needs lots of practice in balance. Pushing a chair or a stroller can help develop his sense of balance.

◆ Find a lightweight chair and show the baby how to push it around the house. While the baby is pushing the chair, recite this poem.

Walking, walking, I am walking,
All around, all around.
Walking, walking, I am walking,
All around the town.

◆ Go outside and let your
baby push the stroller
while you repeat
the poem.

◆ WHAT YOUR BABY WILL LEARN:
BALANCE

High Steps

◆ Play this game when your baby is first learning to walk. Balancing is hard, and this game will help her improve her balance.

◆ Place a few small toys (blocks are good) on the floor.

◆ Hold the baby's hand as she walks. When she reaches the toys, she will have to lift her foot in order to step over them.

◆ Show the baby how to march. She will enjoy this, and it is excellent for her muscle development.

◆ Once the baby can step over the blocks easily, find other blocks or toys or boxes that are just a little higher. This will be a new challenge.

◆ As you both step over the blocks, tell your baby that she is stepping "over" something.

◆ Also try walking "around" the blocks.

WHAT YOUR BABY WILL LEARN:
BALANCE

Find the Bell

◆ You will need three small milk cartons and contact paper.

◆ Cover two cartons with paper of any color of your choice, and the third carton with a different color.

◆ Place a small bell or other noisemaker inside the third carton. Seal all three cartons **securely**.

◆ Give the baby a carton and help him shake it.

◆ When you give him the carton that makes noise when shaken, react to the noise, so he will react as well.

◆ Help your baby learn to discriminate color by choosing the carton that has a sound inside.

◆ WHAT YOUR BABY WILL LEARN:
ABOUT SOUNDS AND COLORS

Chasing Balls

◆ Chasing a ball and returning it is wonderful exercise.

◆ Find a beach ball and roll it down a hill. Tell your baby to go get the ball. When he gets the ball, show him how to push it back to you or, if he is walking, he can carry it back.

◆ Once you play this game, your child will want to do it over and over.

◆ Try throwing a ball against a wall so that it bounces back to the baby. He will delight in trying to retrieve it.

◆ Give the ball to the baby and see what he does with it. If he tries to imitate you, chase the ball and bring it back to him.

◆ **WHAT YOUR BABY WILL LEARN:**
TO PLAY WITH A BALL

Lots of Shoes

◆ Collect several pairs of shoes.

◆ Take one shoe and pile the rest on the opposite side of the room.

◆ Give the shoe to your baby and tell her to find the other one in the pile.

◆ If she has trouble, help her find the other one. Talk about something on the shoes to help her understand that they go together, like a tassel, a certain design, color, shape, etc.

◆ Give her another shoe from the pile and see whether she can match it. With practice, your baby will be able to do this very easily.

◆ WHAT YOUR BABY WILL LEARN:
MATCHING SKILLS

Give Me the Toy

◆ Pick three of your baby's favorite toys.

◆ Hold each toy in your hand and say its name.

◆ Put all three toys in front of your baby. Name one of the toys and ask the baby to give it to you.

◆ When he picks the right one, clap and praise him enthusiastically.

◆ Put one of the toys behind your back. Ask him where the toy is, then bring it out from behind your back.

◆ Put the same toy behind the baby's back. Ask him where the toy is. Soon he will understand that the toy is behind his back.

◆ WHAT YOUR BABY WILL LEARN:
LANGUAGE SKILLS

Special Bonding Games

Special Times

◆ Newborns respond to touch and sound. Each time you pick up your baby and speak to her, you are establishing trust between the two of you.

◆ The tone of your voice and the strength of your arms become familiar to your infant.

◆ Be consistent in the way you hold your baby, the things that you say to her and the tone of your voice.

◆ Soon your baby will coo and smile at you. This is her way of communicating her love.

◆ WHAT YOUR BABY WILL LEARN:
TRUST

Talking Toys

◆ Find a quiet time to play this game with your baby.

◆ Place a variety of stuffed toys and animals around the crib. Some should be small enough for the baby to grasp.

◆ Hold a toy in front of the baby and move it around. As you move the toy, make it "talk" by saying, "Hi, baby," "How are you baby?" etc.

◆ The baby will try to grasp the toy. When she grasps the toy, she will feel successful.

◆ Do this game with toys of many sizes, shapes and textures. Vary your voice when you make the toy talk. This gives the baby an opportunity to hear different sounds.

◆ This is an excellent game for developing small motor and listening skills.

 WHAT YOUR BABY WILL LEARN: LANGUAGE SKILLS

Coos and Hugs

♦ The language of infants is cooing. When an infant sees something of interest, he responds with a coo.

♦ Play a cooing game with your baby. Hold a brightly colored object in front of the baby's eyes. When the baby responds with a coo, answer him with a coo and a hug.

♦ You will soon find out what pleases your baby.

♦ When babies learn that their sounds please another person, they will make more sounds. This encourages early language development and talking.

WHAT YOUR BABY WILL LEARN:
LANGUAGE SKILLS

Kick, Kick, Kick

◆ Babies enjoy kicking and lifting their legs. As you well know, they get their toes into their mouths at a very young age.

◆ To help your baby practice kicking, place items at the baby's feet such as stuffed animals, your hand, squeaky toys, etc.

◆ Place one item at a time at your baby's feet.

◆ Hold a pillow at the baby's feet and let him kick it.

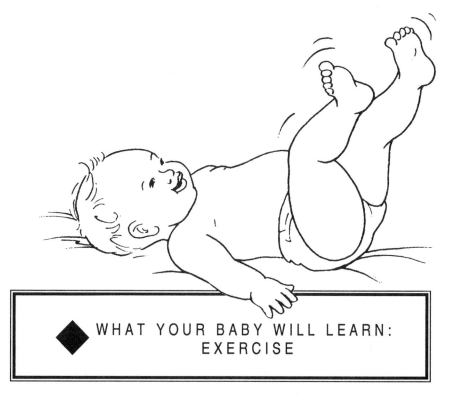

◆ WHAT YOUR BABY WILL LEARN:
EXERCISE

I See You

◆ Lie on your back and put your baby on your tummy. Call her name and raise her slightly to encourage her to lift her head to see you.

◆ Repeat this game over and over with praise for the baby each time she lifts her head a little bit.

◆ Try the same game by putting the baby on the floor on her tummy. Hold a brightly colored object in front of her to encourage her to lift her head.

◆ Each time she lifts her head a little, praise her.

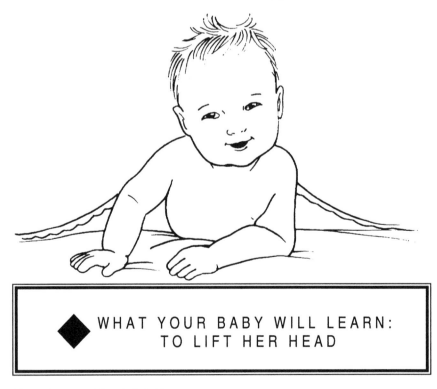

◆ WHAT YOUR BABY WILL LEARN:
TO LIFT HER HEAD

Stroke the Baby

◆ This is a wonderful bonding game that encourages loving interaction with an adult.

◆ Find a variety of objects with which to stroke your baby. A blanket, silk, a feather or a cotton ball are all excellent.

◆ Hum softly as you stroke the baby. Lullabies are nice.

◆ Rub the baby's fingers and toes one at a time as you hum. The baby will enjoy this very much.

◆ Next stroke the baby's fingers and toes one at a time with each object.

 WHAT YOUR BABY WILL LEARN:
BONDING

Puppet Games

◆ Put a finger puppet on your index finger. Moving it around, say the baby's name.

◆ Move the puppet up and down, and see whether the baby can follow the movement.

◆ Try moving the puppet in a circle.

◆ Each time that the baby is able to follow the movement, try a new movement.

◆ WHAT YOUR BABY WILL LEARN:
TO WATCH AN OBJECT

Necklace for Baby

◆ Find a colorful necklace or string colored beads to wear around your neck.

◆ Wear the necklace when you are feeding or nursing your baby.

◆ While the baby rests, she will have something colorful to look at.

◆ If you jiggle the necklace, the baby will become more interested.

◆ Looking at the colors while hearing your soothing voice, will bring much satisfaction and happiness to your baby.

 WHAT YOUR BABY WILL LEARN: ABOUT COLORS

Baby Boop

◆ This is a good game to play while changing your baby's diaper.

◆ Lay the baby on his back. Touch the baby's body in different places and make the sound "boop" with each touch.

◆ Your baby may smile each time you touch him and visibly anticipate the next touch in a new place.

◆ When you make the "boop" sound, also name the part of the body you touch.

◆ **WHAT YOUR BABY WILL LEARN:**
SOCIAL SKILLS

Can You Remember?

◆ Sit on a chair with your infant in your lap and a table in front of you.

◆ Place your baby's favorite toy on the table where she can see it.

◆ Talk about the toy to your baby. Then pick her up and turn her to face you.

◆ If she turns her head back to look for the toy, praise her and give her the toy.

◆ If your infant is crawling, play this game on the floor. Lay her on her tummy and put the toy in front of her.

◆ Move the toy to one side of her. She will crawl around to find it.

◆ Once the baby begins looking for the toy, it's important to help her find it quickly. This develops her confidence.

 WHAT YOUR BABY WILL LEARN:
CONFIDENCE

Fly, Baby, Fly

◆ Sit on the floor with your baby facing you. Support the baby's body with your hands placed firmly under his arms and around his chest.

◆ Ask your baby, "Are you ready to fly in the sky?" Then say, "Here we go. One, two, threeeee!"

◆ On the count of three, slowly begin lifting the baby as you roll backward onto your back.

◆ You are now lying down and holding the baby "high in the sky." Say, "Fly, baby, fly!" "Whee," and whatever else you can think of.

◆ This game is very good for the caregiver because it strengthens your back muscles.

◆ WHAT YOUR BABY WILL LEARN:
BONDING

Up Goes the Baby

◆ Hold your baby in your arms and say:

Up, up, up goes the baby.
  (Hold the baby high in the air)
Give a hug to the baby.
  (Hug the baby)
Down, down, down goes the baby.
  (Bring the baby down close to the ground)
Give a hug to the baby.
  (Hug the baby)

◆ When you hug the baby, you might want to sneak in an extra kiss!

WHAT YOUR BABY WILL LEARN:
BONDING

Exploring

◆ Lie on the bed and place the baby on your chest.

◆ Hold the baby firmly and say loving things like "I love you," "What a sweet baby," etc.

◆ Help the baby explore the parts of your body. When the baby touches your nose, say the word "nose." When the baby touches your hair, say the word "hair."

◆ Hold the baby up over your head and say loving things while you look into each other's eyes.

◆ WHAT YOUR BABY WILL LEARN:
EXPLORATION SKILLS

Bumping Noses

◆ Sit the baby in your lap facing you and say "boo" three times.

◆ When you say the first and second "boo," move your head toward the baby's. On the third "boo," bump noses with the baby. If you say the last "boo" a little louder, it makes the game even more fun.

◆ Repeat this over and over. Change the tone of your voice each time. Sometimes use a high voice, and sometimes use a low voice.

◆ Try whispering the first and second "boo," saying the third in a normal voice. Be careful not to shout as this might scare the baby.

◆ WHAT YOUR BABY WILL LEARN:
FUN

Twinkle, Twinkle

◆ One of the first things that infants learn is to recognize sounds. Helping your baby differentiate the sounds she hears will further her development.

◆ Hold your baby in your arms and sing the song "Twinkle, Twinkle, Little Star."

> *Twinkle, twinkle, little star,*
> *How I wonder what you are.*
> *Up above the earth so high,*
> *Like a diamond in the sky.*
> *Twinkle, twinkle, little star,*
> *How I wonder what you are.*

◆ Sing the song in different voices, sometimes high, sometimes low.

◆ Change the baby's position as you sing to her: over one shoulder, then the other shoulder, etc.

WHAT YOUR BABY WILL LEARN:
ABOUT SOUNDS

The Kissy Game

◆ Hold your baby in your arms and recite this following poem, kissing the parts of the body named as you sing each line.

Kissy, kissy fingers,
Kissy, kissy toes,
Kissy, kissy baby,
On your kissy nose.

I love to kiss your fingers,
I love to kiss your toes,
I love to kiss my baby,
On your kissy nose.

◆ WHAT YOUR BABY WILL LEARN:
BODY AWARENESS

The Name Game

◆ Hold your baby in your lap. Touch different features of her face and name each one.

◆ Touch two features. Each time say, "This is baby's (use child's name) nose," "This is baby's cheek." Repeat several times.

◆ Take the baby's hand and touch your nose and cheek alternately. As you guide her hand, say, "This is Daddy's nose," "This is Daddy's cheek."

◆ If you touch and name only two features at a time, it is much easier for the baby to begin to understand.

◆ Now ask the baby, "Where's your nose?" Place her hand on her nose and say, "Here it is!" Keep repeating with all of the features that you have been named.

◆ WHAT YOUR BABY WILL LEARN:
BODY AWARENESS

Which Hand Is It?

◆ Close your hand around a small interesting object.

◆ Open your hand to show the baby. Close your hand.

◆ Ask the baby, "Where's the (name of object)?" Open your hand again to show the object to the baby.

◆ Using your other hand, repeat the game.

◆ Soon your baby will grab your hand to try to reach the object.

◆ This game helps babies understand that objects placed inside containers do not disappear.

◆ WHAT YOUR BABY WILL LEARN:
EXPLORATION SKILLS

Tell Me a Story

◆ Sit the baby in your lap facing you.

◆ Tell him that you have a story to tell.

◆ Begin by saying, "Once upon a time, there was a ...."
Wait for the baby to respond with a coo or a giggle.

◆ Weave into your story events or people familiar to your
baby. Say short sentences and pause to let the baby
respond in his language.

◆ The baby will soon learn that his sounds will elicit a
favorable response from you.

◆ Games like this encourage babies to talk.

◆ **WHAT YOUR BABY WILL LEARN:
LANGUAGE SKILLS**

Feels Good

◆ Hold the baby in your arms and take a texture walk through the house.

◆ Let your baby feel objects as you name their texture.

◆ Find and describe objects that are rough, slick, smooth, soft, hard, prickly, silky, bumpy, and cool. Examples are:

Carpet—soft
Refrigerator—cool
Floor—hard
Stuffed toy—smooth
Scarf—silky

 WHAT YOUR BABY WILL LEARN:
ABOUT TEXTURES

Special Book

◆ Gather together photographs of family, friends, pets and anything else with which your baby is familiar.

◆ Glue each photo on a separate index card. Cover the whole photo with contact paper to protect it.

◆ Punch a hole at the top left-hand corner of each card and thread string, yarn or any sturdy cord through all the holes to bind the cards into a book.

◆ Sit with your baby and talk about each picture. Identify the person and tell the baby something about that person.

◆ Ask the baby to find a certain picture. "Where's Daddy?" "Where's Aunt Mary?"

◆ Your baby will delight in seeing so many familiar faces.

◆ WHAT YOUR BABY WILL LEARN:
LANGUAGE SKILLS

Whoops, Johnny

◆ Take your baby's hand in yours.

◆ Starting with her pinky, touch each of her fingers with your index finger and say the word "Johnny." Keep saying "Johnny" until you reach her index finger.

◆ Slide your finger down her index finger and up the thumb saying, "Whoops." When you reach the tip of the thumb say, "Johnny."

◆ The game will sound like this:

> *Johnny, Johnny, Johnny, Johnny,*
> *Whoops Johnny,*
> *Whoops Johnny,*
> *Johnny, Johnny, Johnny.*

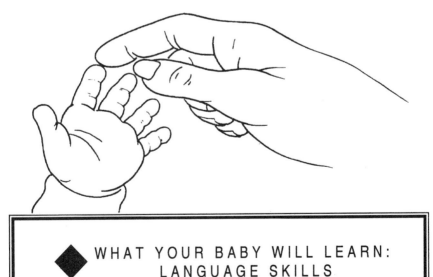

◆ **WHAT YOUR BABY WILL LEARN:**
LANGUAGE SKILLS

Object Hide-and-Seek

◆ Sit on the floor with your baby near a hiding place like a chair or sofa.

◆ Show the baby a toy and let him hold it.

◆ Take the toy away and say, "Now I'm going to hide the toy." While the baby is watching, hide the toy behind the couch.

◆ Ask the baby to find the toy. If the baby does not understand at first, retrieve the toy and try the game again.

◆ Keep playing this game until the baby can find the toy easily.

WHAT YOUR BABY WILL LEARN:
LANGUAGE SKILLS

M-m-m Nice

◆ Put the baby in a sitting position.

◆ Stock a "feely box" with materials of varied texture, and set it aside.

◆ Remove a piece of fur and pat the baby's cheek with it. Rub it along her arms and legs to demonstrate stroking.

◆ As you stroke the baby with the fur, murmur softly, "m-m-m nice," or "so, so soft" or similar words.

◆ Give the baby the fur and let her experiment with it.

◆ Encourage her to pet, stroke or rub it against her.

◆ Use tissue paper to demonstrate crushing and foam rubber for squeezing.

 **WHAT YOUR BABY WILL LEARN:
ABOUT TEXTURES**

The Elbow Game

◆ Get your baby's attention. Hold your elbow in front of your face and say, "Where's Daddy?"

◆ Take your elbow away and say, "Here I am."

◆ Repeat this several times until the baby begins to try to move your elbow away from your face.

◆ Hold a stuffed animal or doll and pretend the doll is saying, "Where's Daddy?" This adds another element to the game, making even more fun.

◆ Try changing your voice each time you say, "Where's Daddy?"

◆ **WHAT YOUR BABY WILL LEARN:**
FUN

Kitchen Games

Peas Porridge Hot

◆ This is a great kitchen game that will develop your child's sense of rhythm.

◆ Recite this popular children's rhyme while clapping baby's hands together.

> *Peas porridge hot, peas porridge cold,*
> *Peas porridge in the pot, nine days old.*
>
> *Some like it hot, some like it cold,*
> *Some like it in the pot, nine days old.*

◆ Touch baby's nose with your finger on "old."

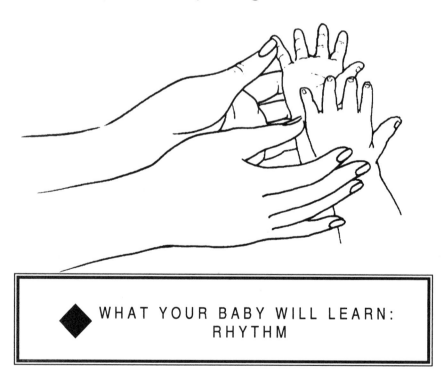

◆ WHAT YOUR BABY WILL LEARN:
RHYTHM

Touching Time

◆ When your baby is feeding, it is important to hold and cuddle him.

◆ The baby's arms and hands should be free for touching and exploring as he feeds.

◆ Place your baby's hands on your face. Move his hands across your nose, mouth, hair and eyes.

◆ Hold and massage his hands gently.

◆ Stroke his arms and talk to him softly.

 WHAT YOUR BABY WILL LEARN:
BONDING

Oh, How Pretty!

◆ When you feed your baby, put a pretty colored towel or scarf over your shoulder.

◆ The baby will enjoy looking at your face and at the towel.

◆ When the baby is through feeding, move the towel in front of her eyes and say soothing words like, "pretty towel, pretty baby."

◆ The next time the baby sees the towel over your shoulder, she will associate it with pleasure.

WHAT YOUR BABY WILL LEARN:
EXPLORATION SKILLS

Find the Noise

◆ After your baby has finished eating, hold him in your lap and play this game.

◆ Shake a rattle on one side of his head, then on the other side.

◆ Try shaking it slowly at first, then faster and faster.

◆ Your baby will search for the noise with his eyes. When you see him responding to the sound, praise him and cuddle him.

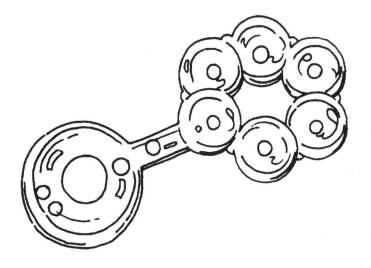

◆ WHAT YOUR BABY WILL LEARN:
ABOUT SOUNDS

Here's the Spoon!

◆ When your baby first sees a spoon, she may not know what it is for.

◆ Show her the spoon without any food. Say something nice to her so that she will associate spoons with enjoyment.

◆ Hold the spoon in front of her, raise it to your mouth and pretend to eat, saying, "Yum, yum, yum."

◆ Now place some food in the spoon and hold it to your baby's mouth. Feed her the food.

◆ Soon she will understand what the spoon is for, and become very excited each time she sees it.

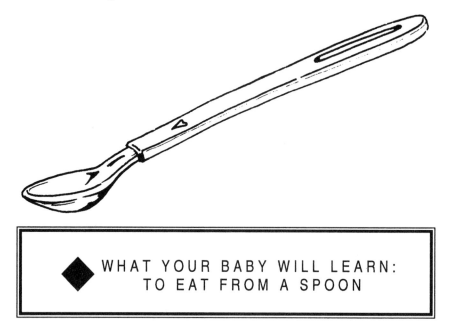

◆ WHAT YOUR BABY WILL LEARN:
TO EAT FROM A SPOON

Hand Fun

◆ When your baby is able to sit comfortably in a high chair, you can start giving him small bits of food to pick up.

◆ Dry cereal and diced cooked vegetables will challenge your baby and develop his dexterity.

◆ Put some dry cereal on the baby's high chair and show him how to pick one up and put it down again. (Putting it down is the hard part.)

◆ Show your baby how to pick up and place a piece of food in the other hand.

◆ Hold out your hand, palm up, and see if your baby can pick up and place a piece of food and in your hand.

 WHAT YOUR BABY WILL LEARN:
HAND-EYE COORDINATION

Cockle Doodle Doo

◆ Children love this game because of the words "cockle doo-dle doo."

> *All around the kitchen,*
> *Cockle doodle doo.*
> *All around the kitchen,*
> *Cockle doodle doo.*
> *Put your hand on your head,*
> *Cockle doodle doo.*
> *Put your hand on your ear,*
> *Cockle doodle doo.*
> *Put your hand on your nose,*
> *Cockle doodle doo.*
> *Put your hand on your cheek,*
> *Cockle doodle doo.*

◆ Hold your baby as you say the words and put his hand on the parts of the body that you mention.

◆ Name things in the kitchen and place your baby's hand on them.

> *Put your hand on your bottle....*
> *Put your hand on the table....*
> *Put your hand on the spoon....*

◆ **WHAT YOUR BABY WILL LEARN:**
BODY AWARENESS

Jelly in the Bowl

◆ Playing with Jell-O® is a wonderful way to introduce babies to texture.

◆ Mix Jell-O® and let it set. Cut it into blocks and put them on your baby's tray. She will love watching the Jell-O® squirm and move around.

◆ Here is an old and popular rhyme to recite as you play with the Jell-O®.

> *Jelly in the bowl,*
> *Jelly in the bowl,*
> *Wibble wobble, wibble wobble,*
> *Jelly in the bowl.*

◆ Change the word "jelly" to "Jell-O®."

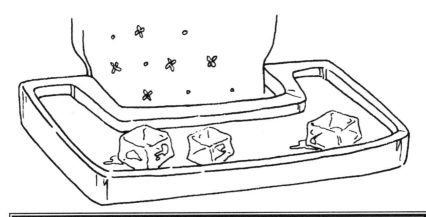

◆ WHAT YOUR BABY WILL LEARN:
EXPLORATION SKILLS

What's Cooking?

◆ Whenever you are in the kitchen, sit your baby safely in an infant seat or swing.

◆ As you prepare food, talk about each thing that you do.

> *"I'm stirring,"*
> *"I'm pouring,"*
> *"I'm washing."*

◆ Let your baby play with measuring spoons, bowls, wooden spoons.

◆ When your baby is old enough, let him help pour, beat, stir.

◆ Always name each ingredient as you use it.

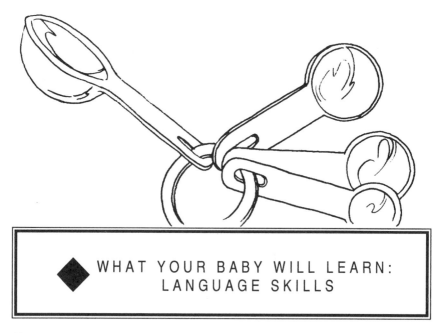

◆ WHAT YOUR BABY WILL LEARN:
LANGUAGE SKILLS

Talk to Me, Baby

◆ When babies first talk, it is called babbling. Babies make all kinds of sounds as they experiment with moving their tongues around in their mouths.

◆ First sounds like "da, da, da" are exciting for parents. When your baby says "da, da, da," answer her with the same sounds.

◆ If you answer the baby, she will probably repeat the sound.

◆ Repeat the sounds the baby makes. This will encourage her to babble more and more, because she enjoys communicating with you.

◆ While you are playing this game, make a new sound and see if the baby will imitate you. Try "mo, mo, mo" or "dee, dee, dee."

 WHAT YOUR BABY WILL LEARN: LANGUAGE SKILLS

Spaghetti Game

◆ Cook spaghetti and place a few strands on the high chair tray.

◆ Show the baby how to move it around. Pick it up, shake it, stroke it and talk about its texture.

◆ Let the baby experiment. Clap and encourage all of his actions.

◆ Stick several pieces of the spaghetti together and let the baby attempt to take them apart.

◆ Try singing "On Top of Spaghetti" as you play this game.

◆ WHAT YOUR BABY WILL LEARN:
CREATIVITY

Cup Games

◆ Sit your baby in a high chair or at a table with a flat surface that she can reach.

◆ Set a small cup in front of her.

◆ Pick up the cup and pretend you are drinking from it, saying words like "yum, yum" or "good, good."

◆ Hold the cup to the baby's mouth and say the same words as she pretends to drink.

◆ Place the cup on the tray. See whether the baby will play the game by herself.

 WHAT YOUR BABY WILL LEARN:
TO DRINK FROM A CUP

Muffin Tin Game

◆ Place a toy in one of the cups of a small muffin tin.

◆ Show the baby how to take the toy out and put it back.

◆ Encourage the baby to take the toy out and put it back.

◆ Put another toy in a second cup and repeat the activity.

◆ Keep adding toys until all the muffin cups are filled.

◆ Your baby will get endless enjoyment out of taking the toys out and putting them back.

◆ WHAT YOUR BABY WILL LEARN:
FUN

Bang It and Shake It

◆ Play this game when the baby is alert.

◆ Sit the baby in a high chair or on an uncarpeted floor.

◆ Attract the baby's attention by banging a block on the table or floor. Encourage the baby to do the same, and express your delight at his attempt.

◆ Repeat this activity by shaking a rattle.

◆ Once the baby gets the idea of holding onto an object while shaking or banging, it's nice to sing a song along with him.

◆ A nursery rhyme like "Mary Had a Little Lamb" or "The Farmer in the Dell" works very well.

 WHAT YOUR BABY WILL LEARN:
TO SHAKE AN OBJECT

Pots and Pans

◆ Babies love to play with pots and pans.

◆ Show the baby how to put a lid on a pot.

◆ After the baby can put the lid on without any problem, add a second lid of a different size.

◆ See if the baby can solve the problem of which lid to put on the pot.

◆ Put small toys or edible food inside the pot. When the baby takes off the lid, she will find a surprise.

◆ WHAT YOUR BABY WILL LEARN:
PROBLEM-SOLVING SKILLS

The Napkin Game

◆ Babies adore this game and will play it for long periods.

◆ Sit the baby on your lap facing you.

◆ Place a dinner napkin of soft material on your head, partially covering your face.

◆ Take the napkin off and say "peek-a-boo."

◆ Do this several times before trying it on the baby. Then put the napkin on the baby's head, pull it off and say "peek-a-boo."

◆ Put the napkin on the baby's head and see if she will pull it off herself. Keep pulling it off until she learns to do it herself.

◆ WHAT YOUR BABY WILL LEARN:
A SENSE OF HUMOR

The Spoon Game

◆ Babies love to bang spoons on surfaces or against another spoon.

◆ Give your baby a wooden spoon and show him how to hit it on different surfaces—the table, floor, newspaper, etc.

◆ Give your baby two metal spoons and show him how to bang them together, as well as on different surfaces.

◆ Ask him, "Can you make the spoons go bang?" When he does it, shout, "yeahhhhh!"

◆ Give the baby a pot and show him how to stir the spoon in the pot. This takes a lot of hand-eye coordination.

WHAT YOUR BABY WILL LEARN:
ABOUT SOUNDS

Three Blocks, Two Hands

◆ Put your baby in a high chair or on the floor.

◆ Place two blocks in front of the baby.

◆ If the baby doesn't pick up the blocks, put them in her hand.

◆ Take a third block and give it to the baby. She will learn to drop one block in order to pick up another.

◆ Hand release skills are a very important development.

◆ WHAT YOUR BABY WILL LEARN: TO DROP AN OBJECT

I Can Do It Myself

◆ Put a small piece of cereal or banana on the baby's high chair tray.

◆ Pick up the food and put it in your mouth, saying, "I am picking up the banana and putting it in my mouth. Yum, yum, yum."

◆ Take the baby's hand and help him pick up a piece of banana, saying, "(Child's name) is picking up the banana and putting it in his mouth. Yum, yum, yum."

◆ You may change the word at the end of the sentence from "Yum, yum, yum" to others such as "chew, chew, chew," "good, good, baby," or "oh! boy."

◆ **WHAT YOUR BABY WILL LEARN: TO PICK UP SMALL OBJECTS**

Pouring Game

◆ Pouring is a skill that children will develop with lots of practice.

◆ The kitchen is a good place to practice pouring, and dry cereal is an easy thing to pour.

◆ Place two cups of the same size on the high chair. Put a little cereal in one of the cups and show the baby how to pour it into the other.

◆ As your baby practices, he will enjoy sampling the pieces that drop.

◆ Replace the cups with two of different size. This gives the baby a chance to experiment even further.

 WHAT YOUR BABY WILL LEARN:
TO POUR

Find the Snack

- ◆ You will need three clear plastic glasses and dry cereal or small round crackers.

- ◆ Sit your child in the high chair and, while she is watching, hide a cracker under one of the glasses. Let the child find the cracker and eat it.

- ◆ Keep repeating this game, adding a second glass and then the third. Always be sure that your baby is watching where you hide the cracker.

- ◆ Each time the baby finds the cracker, praise her.

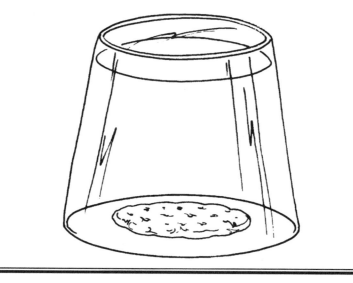

◆ WHAT YOUR BABY WILL LEARN: HAND-EYE COORDINATION

Choo, Choo Food

◆ Tie several milk cartons together with colored yarn to make a train.

◆ Cut out one side of a carton and fill it with dry cereal, raisins or other nutritious finger food.

◆ Show the baby how to pull the carton around the floor.

◆ As you pull, say, "Choo choo food, choo choo food, whooo (like a train whistle), whooo."

◆ Say to the baby, "Let's stop at the station and have a snack." Put a raisin or piece of cereal into your mouth.

◆ Keep playing and encourage the baby to pull the train himself.

◆ WHAT YOUR BABY WILL LEARN:
TO PULL AN OBJECT

Does It Fit?

◆ Learning about size is a hands-on experience for babies. Touching objects and trying to fit one thing into another is the way babies learn about large and small. This happens long before they understand words like "large" and "small."

◆ Graduated measuring cups are excellent toys to use in teaching babies about size.

◆ Give your baby two cups. Put one inside the other for him to see, then let him try placing one inside the other by himself.

◆ When he figures out how to do this, give him a third cup.

◆ While he experiments with the sizes, praise him and let him know what a good job he is doing.

WHAT YOUR BABY WILL LEARN:
ABOUT DIFFERENT SIZES

Stack Them Up

◆ Save containers used in your kitchen: cereal boxes, margarine containers, egg cartons, milk cartons, juice cans, plastic bottles.

◆ Let your baby experiment with stacking the containers. She will learn a lot about balance.

◆ Show your baby how to build a tower using the containers. When it topples over, laugh with her so she understands that it's okay for it to fall down.

◆ Make a bridge or a tunnel with the containers and show her how to push a car across the bridge or through the tunnel.

◆ WHAT YOUR BABY WILL LEARN: BALANCE

It's Cold

♦ When you take your baby to the supermarket, each time you purchase an item that is cold, show it to him and let him feel it while you say the word "cold."

♦ When you get home, leave the cold items out on the counter.

♦ Open the refrigerator and let the baby feel inside. Tell him that it is cold.

♦ Hand him the cold items that he can hold and ask him to put them in the refrigerator. As he does so, say, "Thank you for putting away the cold cheese," naming each item and using the word cold each time.

WHAT YOUR BABY WILL LEARN:
A SENSE OF TOUCH

Laughing and Having Fun Games

Mouth Noises

◆ Imitate the noises that your baby makes with her mouth. This will establish wonderful communication between you and your baby.

◆ Try the following suggestions.

Kissing
Tongue clicking
The raspberry
A "ch ch" sound
Stick your index finger in your mouth and pop it out.
Blowing out and sucking in air.
Make a "bub bub" sound by moving your lips up and
    down with your index finger while humming.

◆ **WHAT YOUR BABY WILL LEARN:**
LANGUAGE SKILLS

Seeing the World

◆ Tuck a pillow under your baby's chest. This makes it easier for her to hold up her head and look around.

◆ Arrange interesting toys in front of the baby.

◆ Prop a mirror in front of her so that she can watch "another baby."

◆ While a baby lies flat on her stomach, her world is limited. While she is propped up, her hands can explore and touch.

◆ While your baby is propped up, tell her about all the things that she can see.

◆ WHAT YOUR BABY WILL LEARN: OBSERVATION SKILLS

Follow the Bee

◆ Sit in a comfortable chair holding your baby in your arms.

◆ Hold your finger in the air and make a buzzing sound.

◆ Move your finger around as you buzz.

◆ The baby's eyes will follow the "bee." Land the "bee" on the baby with a slight tickle.

◆ Repeat this many times.

◆ Now, hold the baby's finger in the air. Move it around as you did your finger and land it on your cheek.

◆ Babies enjoy this very much.

◆ WHAT YOUR BABY WILL LEARN:
OBSERVATION SKILLS

Tickle Cheek

◆ There is nothing more delightful than a smiling baby. This game will encourage your baby to smile a lot.

◆ Rock your baby back and forth in your arms very gently.

◆ Stroke the skin near his mouth softly with your index finger.

◆ When he smiles at you, praise him and let him know how pleased you are.

◆ Try this game. Stroke the baby's face three times, then say, "smile." As you stroke his face count to three. "One, two, three....smile."

◆ WHAT YOUR BABY WILL LEARN:
FUN

Exercise Fun

◆ This game will tone your baby's muscles and help develop her sense of rhythm.

◆ Put your baby on her back and gently move her arms and legs to the rhythm of a nursery rhyme.

◆ Say the words to "Baa, Baa, Black Sheep" as you move her hands in a circle.

◆ Say the words to "Diddle, Diddle, Dumpling" as you move the baby's legs back and forth.

◆ WHAT YOUR BABY WILL LEARN:
EXERCISE

Tongue Fun

◆ Infants will imitate the faces and sounds that you make.

◆ Hold the baby and get his attention.

◆ Stick out your tongue and make a noise at the same time.

◆ Your baby will try to imitate you by opening his mouth and putting his tongue out too.

◆ Try moving your tongue up and down and side to side, and see what your baby does!!

◆ WHAT YOUR BABY WILL LEARN:
IMITATION

Squeaky Toys

◆ Sit in a chair with your baby in your lap.

◆ Squeeze a squeaky toy.

◆ Place the toy in the baby's hand. She will grasp it as a natural reflex and be surprised when it squeaks.

◆ Keep giving her the toy, and soon she will realize that her hand makes the toy squeak.

◆ WHAT YOUR BABY WILL LEARN:
BODY AWARENESS

Roll Little One, Roll

◆ When your baby first rolls over, he usually cannot roll back. When this happens in the middle of the night, this newly acquired skill doesn't seem so great.

◆ Play this game with your baby in order to practice rolling over and back.

◆ Make up any tune to this song. As you sing, roll your baby from his tummy to his back.

> *Roll, roll, little one, roll*
> *From your tummy to your back.*
> *Roll, roll, little one, roll*
> *When you go over, you must come back.*

◆ Practice rolling over may prevent the middle of the night problem.

 WHAT YOUR BABY WILL LEARN:
TO ROLL OVER

Reach Out and Touch

◆ Tie a scarf around your neck so that the ends dangle in front of you.

◆ Lean over your baby so that she can see your face and reach the scarf.

◆ Slowly shake the scarf to attract her attention. Touch her hands with the scarf.

◆ As the baby reaches for the scarf, talk to her and smile to let her know that you are happy about what she is doing.

◆ The more you encourage the baby, the more confident she will feel.

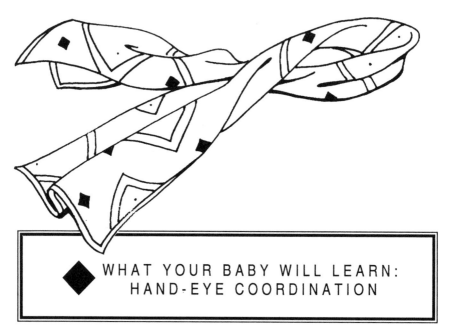

◆ WHAT YOUR BABY WILL LEARN:
HAND-EYE COORDINATION

Balance Game

◆ Lay the baby next to you on a bed. Push gently on the mattress to make it bounce.

◆ Hold the baby firmly under his arms and bounce him up and down on the bed.

◆ Lie beside the baby and make the mattress bounce while cuddling the baby and talking to him.

◆ This game stimulates a baby's sense of balance.

 WHAT YOUR BABY WILL LEARN:
BALANCE

Bouncy Bouncy

◆ Sit on a comfortable chair with your legs crossed.

◆ Sit the baby on your legs and grasp him under the arms.

◆ Move your legs up and down and recite this rhyme.

Bouncy, bouncy baby.
Bouncy, bouncy baby.
Up and down, up and down,
Bouncy, bouncy baby.

Hippety hop, bippety bop,
Bouncy, bouncy BOOM.

◆ When you say, "BOOM," lift the baby up for a big hug.

◆ WHAT YOUR BABY WILL LEARN:
BALANCE

One, Two, Three

◆ Play this game on the bed. Lay your baby on her back on a pillow facing you.

◆ Grasp the baby's hands and begin counting.

> *Are you ready to stand up? Here we go!*
> *One, (pronounced "wwwwuuuunnnn")*
> *Two, (pronounced "toooooo")*
> *Three, (pronounced "threeeee")*

◆ On the count of three, gradually pull the baby to a standing position without letting go of her hands.

◆ Your baby will think this is great fun and will easily learn to count to three.

◆ The baby will also learn to anticipate something fun happening whenever the count of three is reached.

WHAT YOUR BABY WILL LEARN:
TO STAND UP

The Spider Game

◆ This game is a lot of fun.

◆ You and the baby lie on the floor on your tummies, facing each other.

◆ Make your fingers crawl like a spider. Make them disappear and reappear. Wiggle your fingers.

◆ Recite this poem, acting out the words with your hand.

See the little spider crawling right by you.
Here it comes!
There it goes!
Good-bye spider, come again sometime.
Hello, spider on your hand.
Hello, spider on your nose.
Good-bye spider!

◆ WHAT YOUR BABY WILL LEARN:
ANTICIPATION

Here Comes a Bug

◆ Sit your baby in a chair or on the floor facing you.

◆ Wiggle your fingers across the chair or floor, closer and closer to the baby.

◆ As you are wiggling say, "Here comes the bug, buggy, buggy, bug."

◆ When you get close to the baby, "jump" your fingers onto his toe or finger.

◆ Say the word "jump" as your hand leaps toward him.

 WHAT YOUR BABY WILL LEARN:
ANTICIPATION

I'm Gonna Get You

◆ Repetitive games help infants learn how to take turns.

◆ Hold your baby and say, "I'm gonna get you," then nuzzle her tummy with your head.

◆ Repeat this game over and over again. The baby will get much pleasure out it.

WHAT YOUR BABY WILL LEARN:
ANTICIPATION

Silly Sounds

◆ Sit your baby in your lap facing you.

◆ Make funny sounds and shapes with your mouth:

> *Shape your lips like a fish and smack them.*
> *Stick out your tongue and wiggle it.*
> *Shape your mouth into a circle and make a*
> *   funny sound.*

◆ These sights and sounds will make your baby laugh. He will also try to imitate you.

WHAT YOUR BABY WILL LEARN:
IMITATION

Head and Shoulders

◆ Lay the baby on his back while you play this game. Sing to the tune of "London Bridge Is Falling Down."

> *Head and shoulders, knees and toes,*
> *Knees and toes, knees and toes.*
> *Head and shoulders, knees and toes,*
> *I love my baby.*
>
> *Eyes and ears and mouth and nose,*
> *Mouth and nose, mouth and nose.*
> *Eyes and ears and mouth and nose,*
> *I love my baby.*

◆ Touch each part of the body as you name it in the song.

WHAT YOUR BABY WILL LEARN:
BODY AWARENESS

Little Mouse

◆ Open your baby's hand and circle your finger on her palm.

◆ As you move your finger, say:

> *Little mouse, little mouse goes around.*
> *Little mouse, little mouse goes to town.*

◆ Walk your finger up the baby's arm and tickle her under the chin.

◆ Try playing this game with the baby's toes. When the mouse goes to town, walk your finger up the baby's leg to her tummy.

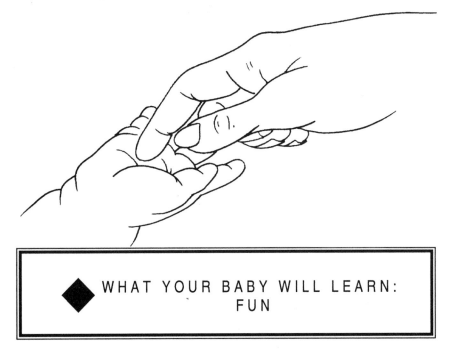

WHAT YOUR BABY WILL LEARN:
FUN

Where's the Mousie?

◆ Hold your baby with his head over your shoulder.

◆ Starting at the baby's waist, walk your fingers up his back to his shoulder and tickle him under the neck.

◆ As you walk your fingers up his back, say:

Mousie, mousie, where's the mousie?

◆ When you reach the baby's shoulder, and you're ready to tickle him under the neck, say:

Here's the mousie, BOO!

◆ Turn the baby over and hold him in your lap. Play the same game starting at his tummy.

◆ WHAT YOUR BABY WILL LEARN:
FUN

The Paper Game

◆ Collect various kinds of paper—wrapping paper, aluminum foil, tissue paper, etc.

◆ Crumple a piece of paper in your hand.

◆ Give the same kind of paper to the baby and help her crumple it in her hand.

◆ Select a different kind of paper and crinkle it in your hand.

◆ Give this kind of paper to your baby and let her crinkle it.

◆ Crumple the paper and drop it into a paper sack.

◆ Encourage your baby to copy you.

◆ The baby will enjoy not only the various crinkling sounds, but also dropping the crumpled-up paper into a sack.

 WHAT YOUR BABY WILL LEARN: ABOUT SOUNDS

Floor Games

◆ Get down on the floor with your baby and crawl around. See if you can persuade him to crawl with you.

◆ Pretend to be a dog or a cat and say, "woof, woof" or "meow, meow."

◆ Place one or two laundry-sized baskets on the floor filled with the baby's toys. Encourage him to take a toy out of the basket and then put it back.

◆ When the baby takes a toy out of the basket, name the toy: "truck," "ball."

WHAT YOUR BABY WILL LEARN:
TO CRAWL

Mama, Dada

◆ At this age, babies begin to associate language with people and things.

◆ Arrange large photographs of Mommy, Daddy and other relatives who baby knows beside the crib, near the high chair, near the changing area.

◆ When the baby starts making sounds like "dada," point to the picture of Daddy and say, "This is Daddy."

◆ Point to the pictures at other times and use the person's name in a sentence. "Mommy loves you," "Grandma is coming today," and so on.

◆ WHAT YOUR BABY WILL LEARN:
LANGUAGE SKILLS

Father, Mother and Uncle John

◆ Sit your baby in your lap facing you. Hold him firmly but gently. It's easiest to do this while sitting on the floor.

◆ Recite this poem to your baby as you bounce him up and down on your lap.

Father, Mother and Uncle John
Rode to the doctor, one by one.
Father fell off. (Slide the baby to one side)
Mother fell off. (Slide the baby to the other side)
And Uncle John rode on and on.
And on, and on, and on!

◆ WHAT YOUR BABY WILL LEARN:
BALANCE

To Market, To Market

◆ Sit with the baby on your knees facing you. Hold the baby by the waist until she is old enough to hold onto your hands.

> *To market, to market, to buy a fat pig.*
> *Home again, home again, jiggity jig.*
>
> *To market, to market, to buy a fat hog.*
> *Home again, home again, jiggity jog.*
>
> *To market, to market, to buy a new gown.*
> *Home again, home again,*
> *Whoops!! The horse fell down.*

◆ On the first line of each verse—"To market, to market"— bounce your knees up and down like a horse trotting.

◆ On "Whoops!!" straighten your legs and let the baby slide down to your feet.

 WHAT YOUR BABY WILL LEARN:
BONDING

Tug of War

♦ Get on the floor with your baby.

♦ Give him one end of a long sock while you grasp the other.

♦ Gently pull the sock toward you.

♦ Show the baby how to pull the end toward himself.

♦ Tug back and forth while saying:

> *I pull you and you pull me.*
> *Tug of war just you and me.*

♦ Pretend the baby is so strong that he pulls you over.

◆ WHAT YOUR BABY WILL LEARN:
COOPERATION

The Floating Game

◆ Gather together diapers, scarves, cloth belts and anything else that you can throw into the air to float down
slowly.

◆ Sit on the floor with your baby.

◆ Throw the first item into the air. Scarves are good to
begin with. As it floats back down, extend your arms to
catch it.

◆ Throw the scarf into the air again and tell the baby to
catch it. Hold her arms out so that the scarf falls into her
arms.

◆ Continue playing with the different items you selected.
The baby will soon try to catch them herself.

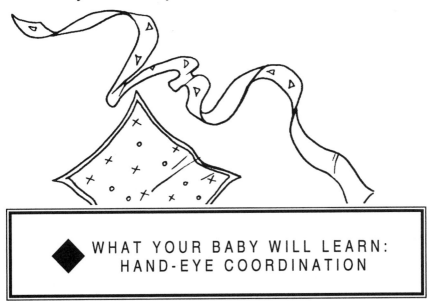

◆ WHAT YOUR BABY WILL LEARN:
HAND-EYE COORDINATION

Where Are Baby's Hands?

◆ Play a hand-clapping game with your baby.

◆ Sit on the floor with the baby facing you.

◆ Lay a blanket over your lap and recite this poem as you clap the baby's hands.

> *Clap your hands, one, two, three,*
> *Play a clapping game with me.*
> *Now your hands have gone away,*
> *Find your hands so we can play.*

◆ When you say, "Now your hands have gone away," move the baby's hands under the blanket.

◆ On "Find your hands so we can play," bring the baby's hands out from under the blanket.

◆ It's fun to pause before saying the last line—it makes for more of a surprise.

WHAT YOUR BABY WILL LEARN:
COORDINATION

Huff and Puff

◆ String a length of twine between the backs of two chairs.

◆ Fold a large piece of tissue paper in half and hang it over the twine to form a "wall."

◆ Cut the tissue paper into vertical strips so that the "wolf" can blow its way into the house.

◆ Tell the story of the "The Three Little Pigs."

◆ When you reach the part where the wolf "huffed and puffed," encourage your child to act out the words.

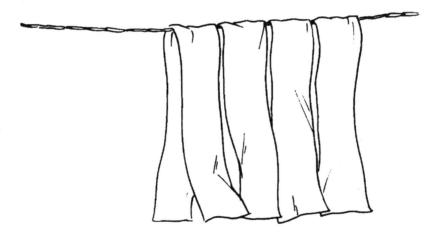

 WHAT YOUR BABY WILL LEARN: LANGUAGE SKILLS

Hats, Hats, Hats

◆ Collect three different hats. Set one hat on your head and say something silly like, "Hello, silly willy."

◆ Place the hat on your baby's head and say the same thing.

◆ Repeat this game with each hat, changing your voice each time you change the hat.

◆ Give the hat to the baby and let him try to put it on his head.

◆ This is a very good game to teach your baby more about his body.

◆ Looking in the mirror with hats on your head is fun, too.

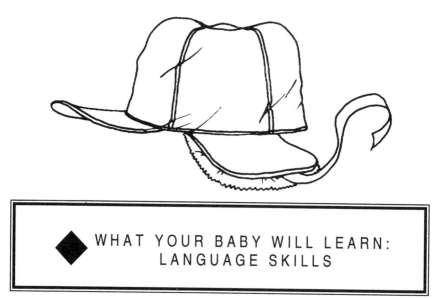

◆ **WHAT YOUR BABY WILL LEARN:**
LANGUAGE SKILLS

Where's the Music?

◆ Play this game inside or outside. You will need a musical toy or music box.

◆ Wind up the music box or toy and hide it somewhere in the room or yard.

◆ Ask the baby, "Where's the music? Let's go find the music."

◆ Crawl with the baby to a place in the room or yard, for example, to a table. Say to the baby, "Is it here?" Then look and say, "No, it's not here."

◆ Repeat. On the third try, go to the hiding place and say, "Hooray, we found it!"

◆ Hide the music box in the same place and repeat the game. Repeat until the baby knows where to go to find the music.

◆ Next try a new place, and see whether the baby can find it by himself.

 WHAT YOUR BABY WILL LEARN:
LISTENING SKILLS

Copy Me

◆ Sit on the floor with your baby and gesture for her to copy.

Tap the floor with your hands.
Stick out your tongue and make silly sounds.
Put a hat on your head.
Open and close your fists.
Wiggle your fingers.
Shake your hands.
Shake your head yes and no.
Wave bye-bye.
Make silly sounds.a with your mouth
Wiggle your index finger over your lips.

◆ These are only ideas. What is important is to talk to your baby while you perform these actions.

◆ **WHAT YOUR BABY WILL LEARN:**
LISTENING SKILLs

Stop and Go

◆ Play this game with your baby while he lies on his back.

◆ Move the baby's legs back and forth while you recite. Move the baby's legs according to the directions in the rhyme.

> *You kick and you kick and you kick and STOP.*
> *You kick and you kick and you kick and STOP.*
> *Kick fast,*
> *Kick slow,*
> *You kick and you kick and you kick and STOP.*

◆ This is a great way to learn language, develop listening skills and exercise muscles all at once.

 WHAT YOUR BABY WILL LEARN:
LISTENING SKILLS

Tunnel Fun

◆ Cut off two opposite sides of a large cardboard box.

◆ Turn the box upside down and encourage your baby to crawl through the tunnel.

◆ Position a toy at one end of the box and your baby at the other to encourage her to go after the toy. After she has done this once, she will do it over and over.

◆ Recite this poem as your baby crawls through the tunnel.

Tunnel, tunnel, crawl right through.
Come out here and say, "How do you do!"

WHAT YOUR BABY WILL LEARN:
TO CRAWL

9-12
MONTHS

Let's Play Ball

◆ There are many things that you can do with balls.

◆ Let your baby explore balls of different sizes and textures.

◆ Show the baby how to push a ball while crawling on the floor.

◆ Roll a ball to where your baby is sitting.

◆ Help your baby roll the ball back to you.

◆ Show your baby how to hold a ball in the air and let it drop.

◆ Show the baby how to bounce a ball. As you demonstrate, say, "bounce, bounce ball."

 WHAT YOUR BABY WILL LEARN: TO PLAY BALL

The Toy Chase

◆ Tie a length of string to a small toy that will fit through a toilet paper or paper towel roll. Toys like cars that will roll are best for this game. **NOTE**: Only use toys that are too large for the baby to swallow.

◆ The string should be longer than the tube.

◆ Lower the toy into the tube, then pull it out.

◆ Hide the toy again, then tip it out the other side end.

◆ Your baby will delight in this mystery. Say to the disappearing toy, "Bye-bye, toy."

◆ When the toy reappears, say "Hello, toy."

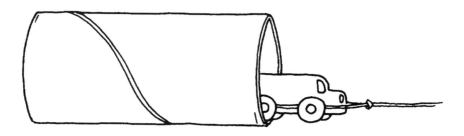

◆ WHAT YOUR BABY WILL LEARN:
HAND-EYE COORDINATION

Upside Down Game

◆ Turn one of your baby's favorite stuffed animals upside down.

◆ Next turn it right side up.

◆ Turn the toy upside down again. Give it to your baby, and see if she can turn it right side up.

◆ Recite this rhyme. On the last line—RIGHT SIDE UP!—turn the animal right side up.

Upside down, upside down,
All the world is upside down.
So get ready, here we go,
RIGHT SIDE UP!!

◆ **WHAT YOUR BABY WILL LEARN:**
TO FOLLOW DIRECTIONS

Silly Stuff

◆ Laughing babies are a joy to behold, and it's fascinating to see what makes them laugh.

◆ Do silly things with your baby, then try to get her to copy you. Here are some ideas.

Take one of your baby's favorite toys and talk babble talk to it.
Pretend to drink from your baby's bottle.
Build a tower with blocks, then knock it down. When you knock it down, say "Uh, oh."
Mess up your hair and make silly sounds as you do it.
Run your fingers up your baby's arm and say, "tickle, tickle."

◆ Observe what makes your baby laugh and think of other things to do.

WHAT YOUR BABY WILL LEARN:
A SENSE OF HUMOR

In the Sky

◆ Sit on the floor with your baby. Raise his arms out to the side.

◆ Flap his arms up and down and tell him he is a bird.

◆ Flap your arms and say, "tweet tweet, tweet tweet, little bird."

◆ Flap your baby's arms, saying the same thing.

◆ Stand up, holding your baby. Stretch one arm outward and pretend that you are an airplane. Make airplane sounds like "zoooom."

◆ Go outside with your baby and look for birds and airplanes. When you see one, flap your arms and say "tweet tweet" or make airplane sounds.

 WHAT YOUR BABY WILL LEARN:
CREATIVITY

Make a Toy

◆ Babies always have favorite toys and containers.

◆ Gather a few of the toys and containers that your baby loves and string them together to make a pull toy.

◆ Start with two or three objects, maybe a box and a stuffed animal.

◆ Show the baby how to pull the toy and sing to the tune of "Row, Row, Row Your Boat."

> *Pull, pull, pull your toy,*
> *Pull it all around.*
> *Merrily, merrily, merrily, merrily,*
> *See it on the ground.*

◆ Ask your baby if she wants to get more toys to pull. She will probably collect more toys.

◆ WHAT YOUR BABY WILL LEARN:
CREATIVITY

Sticky Game

◆ Tape a large piece of contact paper to the floor with the sticky side up.

◆ Place some of your baby's toys on it.

◆ Ask her to pull the toys off. She will be amazed at how difficult it is. She will feel very proud when she is able to.

◆ Hold your baby's hands while she walks on the sticky paper. She will have to pull her legs up high in order to get each foot off the paper. Give her constant encouragement.

◆ WHAT YOUR BABY WILL LEARN:
SELF-CONFIDENCE

The Cardboard Game

◆ Collect toy cars and other toys with wheels.

◆ Fold a large piece of cardboard in half.

◆ Stand the cardboard up to make a hill for the cars to go down.

◆ Show your baby how to let the car roll down the cardboard hill.

◆ Hold a car or toy in your hand and say, "One, two, three, zoom!" Let the car go down the hill.

◆ See if your baby can learn to wait for the word "zoom" before he releases the car.

◆ WHAT YOUR BABY WILL LEARN:
FUN

Mommy Tunnel

◆ Stand with your legs spread far enough apart for your baby to fit through them.

◆ Hold your baby and move him back and forth between your legs.

◆ Once you have done this a few times, see whether he will crawl or walk through your legs.

◆ Say, "Here comes the choo-choo train through the tunnel. Choo, choo, choo."

◆ When he succeeds in going through the "tunnel," praise him a lot.

◆ Give him a push toy, and see if he will push it through the tunnel.

 WHAT YOUR BABY WILL LEARN:
IMAGINATION

Trampoline Game

◆ Lay on your back and draw your knees up to your stomach. Cross your feet at the ankles.

◆ Rest your baby on top of your lower legs. Bounce your legs up and down.

◆ Move your legs faster and slower as you recite this poem.

>*Bounce, bounce, up and down,*
>*Bounce, bounce all around.*
>*Bounce fast,*
>*Bounce slow,*
>*Bounce, bounce, bounce, bounce, BOOM!*

◆ On the word "BOOM," lift your baby up and bring her to your chest for a big hug.

◆ WHAT YOUR BABY WILL LEARN:
BALANCE

Art and Singing Games

What Can I Look At?

◆ Each time you change your baby's environment, you are giving her an opportunity to look at new things. This will develop her curiosity and awareness.

◆ Hold your baby high so that she can look over your shoulder. Walk around the room and stop at something with a bright color or interesting shape.

◆ Let the baby look at this object for a few minutes. Make up a song (any melody will do), and the baby will understand that this is a pleasing experience.

◆ Here is a sample song:

> *Look, look, look with your pretty little eyes,*
> *Look, look, look all around,*
> *See, see, see with your pretty little eyes*
> *Looking all around.*

◆ When you put your baby down, be sure there is something interesting for her to look at.

WHAT YOUR BABY WILL LEARN:
CURIOSITY

High and Low

◆ One of the newborn's most highly developed abilities is responding to sound, including the difference between high- and low-pitched sounds.

◆ Hold your baby close to you and say her name in a soft, high-pitched voice. For example, "Susie, Susie, I love you."

◆ Next say the same words in a soft, low-pitched voice.

◆ Alternate between high and low several times.

◆ **WHAT YOUR BABY WILL LEARN:**
ABOUT SOUNDS

Black and White

◆ A week after birth, babies can discriminate patterns. Sharply contrasting colors and patterns catch their attention most easily.

◆ Cut white posterboard into 8 1/2 x 11 inch pieces. Draw designs on the posterboard with a wide felt-tip pen.

◆ You might also cut pictures out of magazines and tape them to posterboard.

◆ Arrange the designs and pictures around the crib for the baby to look at.

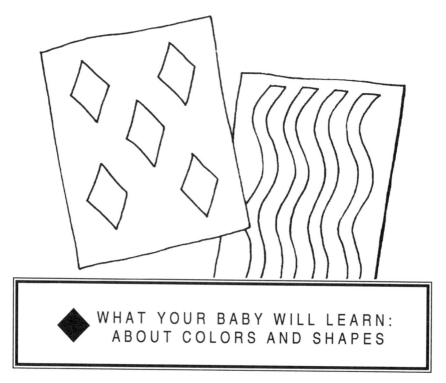

WHAT YOUR BABY WILL LEARN:
ABOUT COLORS AND SHAPES

The Umbrella Mobile

◆ Hang an umbrella upside down at the end of the baby's crib, out of his reach.

◆ Attach colorful balls, small toys or bells to the spokes of the umbrella. **NOTE**: Make certain that the objects are out of baby's reach.

◆ Stand at that end of the crib and talk to the baby. He will follow your voice with his head.

◆ Once you have his attention, jiggle the mobile to encourage him to look at all the colors and shapes.

◆ Once you have done this a few times, the baby will look at the mobile by himself.

WHAT YOUR BABY WILL LEARN:
ABOUT COLORS AND SHAPES

Ride a Cock Horse

◆ Bounce the baby on your lap as you recite this traditional rhyme.

> *Ride a cock-horse, to Banbury Cross,*
> *To see a fine lady upon a white horse.*
> *With rings on her fingers, and bells on her toes,*
> *She shall have music wherever she goes.*

◆ Bounce in a gentle and steady rhythm, and when you get
to the word "goes," lift the baby a little higher in the air.

◆ If you say the last line slowly, and "goes" in a different
voice, it makes the game even more fun.

◆ Your baby will begin to anticipate the word "goes" and
look forward to it with much enthusiasm.

◆ WHAT YOUR BABY WILL LEARN:
LISTENING SKILLS

Sing, Sing, Sing

◆ Sing to your baby about everything. Make up your own tunes and sing about objects in the room, car trips, cleaning. Wherever you are and whatever you are doing can become a song.

◆ Here are some samples that you could sing to the tune of "Row, Row, Row Your Boat."

> *Let's go to the store*
> *On this rainy day.*
> *We will buy some food to eat,*
> *And then go home again.*
>
> *Let's clean up the room,*
> *Lots of things to do.*
> *Make it look so clean and bright,*
> *Now it looks just right.*
>
> *Let's go to the kitchen,*
> *Are you hungry now?*
> *Apples, peas and bread and jelly*
> *And some milk to drink.*

◆ You'll notice that the words do not have to rhyme. It's singing about the tasks that presents a positive attitude and an opportunity to share with your baby.

 WHAT YOUR BABY WILL LEARN: LANGUAGE SKILLS

This Little Piggy

◆ Babies love to play with their fingers and toes. Touch each finger or toe as you recite this poem.

This little piggy went to market,
This little piggy stayed home,
This little piggy had roast beef,
This little piggy had none,
And this little piggy went wee, wee, wee,
All the way home.

◆ Before you say "wee, wee, wee" slow down and build suspense. Then say the last line faster than the rest.

◆ On the "wee, wee, wee," you can do many things. Tickle the baby, dance around holding the baby, or gently shake the baby's hand or foot.

◆ Another variation is to say "wee, wee, wee" in different voices—high, low, happy, sad, and so on.

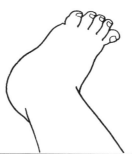

◆ WHAT YOUR BABY WILL LEARN:
BONDING

Are You Sleeping?

◆ A good peek-a-boo song is:

> *Are you sleeping, are you sleeping,*
> *Little (child's name), little (child's name)?*
> *Now it's time to wake up.*
> *Now it's time to wake up.*
> *Ding, ding, dong, ding, ding, dong.*

◆ Lay your baby on the bed and cover your eyes when you say the words, "Are you sleeping, are you sleeping?"

◆ Sing the second line using your child's name. Take your hands away from your eyes.

◆ When you say the words, "Now it's time to wake up," take the baby's hands and gently pull him toward you.

◆ Move the baby's hand up and down as if you were ringing a bell on the words, "Ding, ding, dong."

◆ Another way to sing the song is to put the baby's hands over his own eyes and say the words, "Are you hiding, are you hiding?" The second line would be, "Yes, I am, yes, I am." The rest of the rhyme remains the same.

◆ **WHAT YOUR BABY WILL LEARN:**
BONDING

Where Is Thumbkin?

◆ Babies adore this popular singing game.

Where is Thumbkin?
Where is Thumbkin?
Here I am, here I am.
How are you today, sir?
Very well, I thank you.
Run away, run away.
Where is pointer....Where is tall one....
Where is ring finger....Where is pinky....
Where's the whole family....

◆ Start singing with both hands behind your back. Bring out one thumb when you reach "Here I am." Bring out the other thumb at the second "Here I am."

◆ Wiggle one thumb on the line "How are you today, sir" and wiggle the other thumb on the line "Very well, I thank you."

◆ On the words "Run away," put your thumbs behind your back, one at a time.

◆ Start the second verse with both hands behind your back, and repeat the same actions for each of the fingers: index, middle, ring and pinky. "The whole family" means all five fingers together.

 WHAT YOUR BABY WILL LEARN: DEXTERITY

3-6
MONTHS

The Crawling Game

◆ Get down on the floor with your baby.

◆ Start crawling, and bark like a dog.

◆ Tell your baby to do the same. If she can crawl, crawl next to her. Keep barking like a dog.

◆ Babies love this game and will soon try to make a barking sound like you.

◆ Next make up a tune to the words "crawl, crawl, crawl, boom!"

◆ On the word "boom" fall down and laugh.

◆ Hover over the baby and repeat the same words. On the word "boom," pick up the baby and give him a big hug.

◆ WHAT YOUR BABY WILL LEARN:
FUN

The Dancing Game

◆ Tie a ribbon to the head of a small stuffed toy or a rag doll.

◆ Show the baby how you hold and tug the ribbon to make it dance up and down.

◆ As you dance the doll, move it side to side, back and forth and up and down.

◆ Recite this poem as you dance the doll.

Dance little dolly, dance, dance, dance,
Dance little dolly, dance, dance, dance,
Up and down,
All around,
Dance little dolly, dance, dance, dance.

◆ The baby will enjoy this game very much and will want to try to make the doll dance, too.

◆ WHAT YOUR BABY WILL LEARN:
FUN

Five Little Robins

◆ Recite this poem to your baby. After a few times, he will begin to anticipate which finger you are going to touch.

Five little robins up in a tree.
Father, (Touch baby's thumb)
Mother, (Touch baby's index finger)
And babies three. (Touch the other three
*   fingers)*

Father caught a bug. (Hold up thumb)
Mother caught a worm. (Hold up index finger)
This one got the bug. (Hold up middle finger)
This one got the worm. (Hold up ring finger)
This one said, "Now it's my turn." (Hold up
*   pinkie finger)*

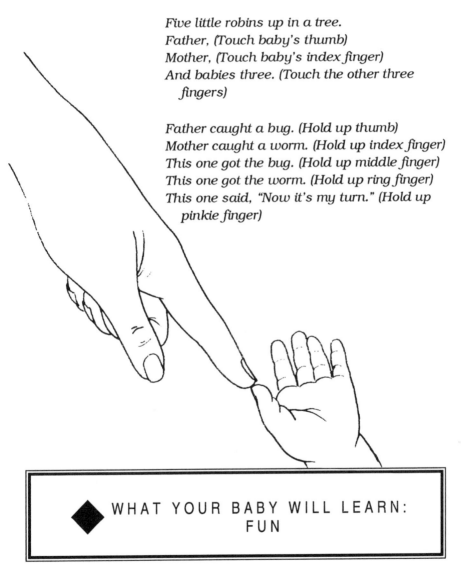

WHAT YOUR BABY WILL LEARN:
FUN

Seesaw

◆ Hold the baby on your lap facing you.

◆ Rock back and forth as you recite the following poem.

> *Seesaw, seesaw,*
> *Back and forth, back and forth.*
> *Seesaw, seesaw,*
> *Up and down, up and down.*
>   *(Lift the baby up and down)*
> *Seesaw, seesaw,*
> *Give a hug, give a hug.*
>   *(Hug the baby)*

◆ Try holding the baby's hands while you "seesaw."

◆ It's easiest to do this while sitting on the floor.

◆ WHAT YOUR BABY WILL LEARN:
FUN

Clap, Clap, Clap

◆ Clap your baby's hands together.

◆ As you clap, say:

> *Clap, clap, clap your hands,*
> *Make a pretty sound.*
> *Clap, clap, clap your hands,*
> *Now you put them down.*
> *(Put hands in lap)*
>
> *Clap them up in the air.*
> *Clap them up on your hair.*
> *Clap, clap, clap your hands,*
> *Make a pretty sound.*

◆ As you say the words, move the baby's hands according to the directions in the poem.

◆ Sing a familiar song with your baby and continue to practice clapping.

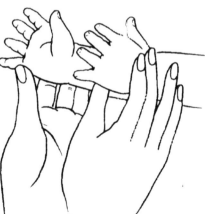

 WHAT YOUR BABY WILL LEARN:
RHYTHM

Making Music

◆ Take a pie pan and a spoon. Hit the spoon on the pie pan a few times.

◆ Give the baby the pie pan and spoon. Help him hit the spoon on the pie pan.

◆ As the baby hits the pie pan, sing a familiar song like "Row, Row, Row Your Boat" or "Mary Had a Little Lamb."

◆ As the baby hits the pie pan, clap your hands and sing.

◆ Babies really love this game, and you will find that she will often play it by herself.

◆ WHAT YOUR BABY WILL LEARN:
RHYTHM

Music Listening

◆ Music can be a wonderful stimulant as well as a very relaxing experience.

◆ Play different kinds of music for your baby.

◆ Hold the baby and dance around to fast music.

◆ Rock the baby gently to soft, slow music.

◆ March with the baby to a strong marching beat.

◆ Bounce the baby on your lap to bouncy, exuberant music.

◆ WHAT YOUR BABY WILL LEARN:
ABOUT SOUNDS

Old MacDonald

◆ Get a set of plastic animals.

◆ As you hold each animal up for the baby, say its name and the make its characteristic sound.

◆ Give the baby each animal after you say its name, and let her feel it. While the baby is holding the animal, repeat its name and the sound it makes.

◆ Sing the song "Old MacDonald Had a Farm."

◆ As you sing each verse, pick up the animal named and move it around.

◆ WHAT YOUR BABY WILL LEARN:
LANGUAGE SKILLS

One, Two, One, Two

◆ Play instrumental music. Holding your baby, sway back and forth as you dance around the room.

◆ Show the baby different ways to move with the music. Clapping hands, stomping feet, swinging arms are a few ideas.

◆ Play vocal music. Sing "La, la, la," and let the baby imitate you. Pick out a particular word in the song and sing it to the baby each time you hear it.

◆ You will be amazed at how quickly the baby will anticipate the word.

◆ Play loud and soft music, fast and slow music, and music that features high and low sounds.

◆ WHAT YOUR BABY WILL LEARN: LISTENING SKILLS

Lazy Mary

◆ Singing this popular children's song is a lovely way to
wake your baby.

> *Lazy Mary, will you get up,*
> *Will you get up, will you get up?*
> *Lazy Mary, will you get up*
> *This cold and frosty morning?*

◆ Substitute the name of your baby for "Mary" and replace
the word "lazy" with words like "pretty," "silly," "funny"
and "happy."

◆ If the baby is lying down while you sing the song, hold
the baby's hands to raise him up gradually.

◆ If you are holding the baby, rock back and forth slowly as
you sing.

WHAT YOUR BABY WILL LEARN:
A MORNING ROUTINE

Humpty Dumpty

◆ Sit your baby on your knees facing you.

◆ Holding your baby's hands, bounce your legs up and down as you say:

> *Humpty Dumpty sat on a wall,*
> *Humpty Dumpty had a great fall.*

◆ On the word "fall," open your legs and gently let the baby down to the floor. When the baby reaches the floor, say "BOOM."

◆ Ask the baby if she wants to do it again. She will love this game and will want to play it over and over.

◆ WHAT YOUR BABY WILL LEARN:
FUN

Two Tube Games

♦ Pretend that a toilet paper tube or a paper towel tube is a microphone.

♦ Hold it to your mouth and sing a familiar song.

♦ Instead of singing through the tube, try making sounds or saying words like your baby does. You might also make announcements through the tube: "Now it's time to play," "Now it's time to eat lunch."

♦ Cut two holes out of a shoe box lid, the size of the tubes that you are using.

♦ The baby can fit the tubes into the holes and take them out again.

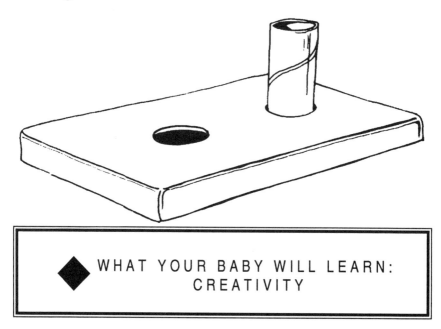

◆ WHAT YOUR BABY WILL LEARN:
CREATIVITY

Singing Fun

◆ Pick three favorite songs that your baby likes to sing. for example, "Twinkle, Twinkle Little Star," "Mary Had a Little Lamb" and "Jingle Bells."

◆ Clap your hands as you sing one of the songs.

◆ Put your baby in your lap and sing the song again, clapping the baby's hands.

◆ Pick a second song, and as you sing, shake bells to the music.

◆ Sing the second song again, this time letting the baby shake the bells.

◆ While you sing a third song, hit a wooden spoon against a metal pot.

◆ Repeat the third song, letting the baby with the spoon.

◆ Your baby will want to play this game again and again.

 WHAT YOUR BABY WILL LEARN:
RHYTHM

Pop Goes the Weasel

◆ Sit your baby in your lap facing you.

◆ Sing "Pop Goes the Weasel" and rock the baby gently back and forth.

> *All around the cobbler's bench,*
> *The monkey chased the weasel.*
> *The monkey laughed to see such fun,*
> *POP, goes the weasel.*

◆ When you come to the word "POP," lift the baby's hands high up in the air.

◆ After you have played this game a few times, your baby will raise her hands when you come to the word "POP."

WHAT YOUR BABY WILL LEARN:
COORDINATION

Finger and Toe Games

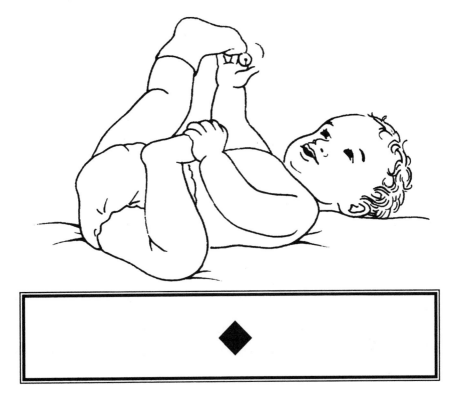

Grass Games

◆ Go outside on a mild day. Spread a blanket on the ground and sit on it with your baby.

◆ Pick a blade of grass and gently stroke the baby on the arm with it.

◆ Turn the baby on her tummy and place the baby's hand on the grass. Move her hand back and forth across it.

◆ The baby will try to grasp the grass and find it very exciting.

WHAT YOUR BABY WILL LEARN:
ABOUT TEXTURES

O-3
MONTHS

Texture Glove

◆ Cover an old glove with materials of different textures. ***NOTE***: Attach all materials securely.

◆ This is easier to do if you secure a different fabric to each finger.

◆ Flannel, silk, velvet and linen work well. Also try attaching a large button or similar large object.

◆ If you cut the fingertips off the gloves, the baby can feel your fingernails as well as the textures of the fabrics.

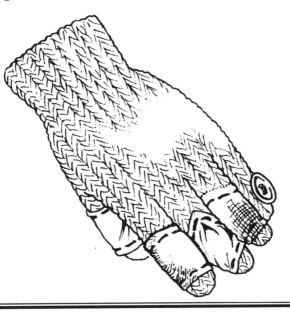

◆ WHAT YOUR BABY WILL LEARN:
ABOUT TEXTURES

Handsy Pansy

◆ Gently stroke your baby's hand with your hand and chant:

> Handsy, pansy,
> Baby's handsy.

◆ Stroke the baby's hand with a soft toy and repeat the chant.

◆ Stroke the baby's hand with your hand and repeat the chant.

◆ Alternate between your hand and toys of different textures.

WHAT YOUR BABY WILL LEARN:
ABOUT TEXTURES

Rattles and Teethers

◆ Play this game when the baby is alert. Seat the baby in a crib or infant seat.

◆ Place a rattle in the baby's hand. The baby may only hold the rattle for a few seconds and then drop it.

◆ Pick up the rattle and give it to the baby again.

◆ Soon the baby will bring the rattle to his mouth. At this stage of development, any object in a baby's hand becomes something for the mouth. You will know when it's time to add a teether.

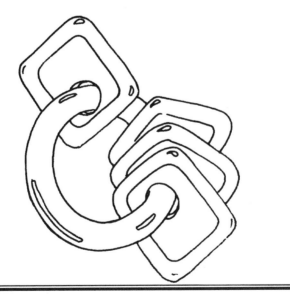

◆ WHAT YOUR BABY WILL LEARN: COORDINATION

Baby Aerobics

◆ Lay your baby on his back. Lift and lower his arms very gently.

◆ Move his arms together and apart very gently.

◆ As you move the baby's arms, recite:

> *Up and down, up and down,*
> *Now we'll move them all around.*
> *Up and down, up and down,*
> *As we do our exercise.*

◆ Repeat the same chant as you move the baby's legs up and down, together and apart.

WHAT YOUR BABY WILL LEARN:
EXERCISE

Dance a Merry Jig

◆ Play this game with either fingers or toes. Alternating them makes your baby become more aware of hands and feet.

◆ Touch one finger or toe at a time as you chant:

This little pig danced a merry, merry jig,
This little pig ate candy.
This little pig wore a blue and yellow wig,
This little pig was a dandy.
But this little pig never grew very big,
And they called her "itty bitty Mandy."
    (Use your child's name)

WHAT YOUR BABY WILL LEARN:
BODY AWARENESS

Baby's Fingers

◆ This game involves lots of touching and helps babies begin to identify parts of their bodies.

◆ Touch the parts of the body that are mentioned in the song as you name them.

◆ With older children, play this game with a doll to reinforce the concepts.

> *Where, oh where, are baby's fingers?*
> *Where, oh where, are baby's toes?*
> *Where's the baby's belly button?*
> *'Round and 'round it goes.*
>
> *Where, oh where, are baby's ears?*
> *Where, oh where, is baby's nose?*
> *Where's the baby's belly button?*
> *'Round and 'round it goes.*

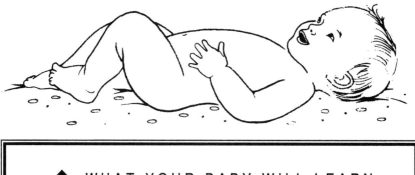

◆ WHAT YOUR BABY WILL LEARN:
BODY AWARENESS

'Round the Mountain

◆ It is important for your baby to exercise her legs.

◆ Lay your baby on her back and cup her feet in the palms of your hands.

◆ Move the baby's legs in and out, then in a circle.

◆ As you move the baby's legs, sing to the tune of "In and Out the Window."

> *Go 'round and 'round the mountain,*
> *Go 'round and 'round the mountain,*
> *Go 'round and 'round the mountain,*
> *And kiss those little toes.*

◆ One the last line, kiss each toe, one by one.

 **WHAT YOUR BABY WILL LEARN:
BODY AWARENESS**

This One's Old

◆ Babies love this traditional Chinese game.

◆ Starting with the baby's thumb or big toe, touch each finger or toe in succession.

> *This one's old,*
> *This one's young,*
> *This one has no meat,*
> *This one's gone to buy some hay,*
> *And this one's gone to the village.*

◆ Adapt this game to fit your environment.

> *This one's old,*
> *This one's young,*
> *This one has a toy,*
> *This one's gone to buy some*
> *(favorite food, etc.),*
> *And this one's gone to the village.*

WHAT YOUR BABY WILL LEARN:
BONDING

Fascinating Toes

◆ Infants love to look at their fingers and toes. This delightful game gives them a new perspective.

◆ Take your baby's sock, plain white preferred, and decorate it with colors, yarn or even attach a bell. **NOTE**: Use
nontoxic materials and fasten them securely.

◆ Put the sock on the baby and watch the excitement that
follows.

◆ Do not leave the baby unattended because he might put
the sock in his mouth.

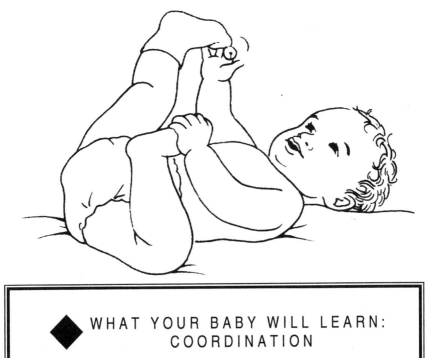

◆ WHAT YOUR BABY WILL LEARN:
COORDINATION

Wiggle Wiggle

◆ Wiggle your index finger in the air as you recite this poem. When you come to the phrase "put it there," touch the baby on the nose.

> *Wiggle, wiggle, wiggle, little finger.*
> *Wiggle, wiggle, wiggle, in the air.*
> *Wiggle, wiggle, wiggle, little finger.*
> *Wiggle all around and put it there.*

◆ Wiggle your fingers in different ways, and the baby will imitate you. Wiggle in front of you, over your head, to one side, etc. Show the baby that there are choices.

◆ Instead of touching the baby's nose, tickle her tummy or touch another part of her body.

◆ **WHAT YOUR BABY WILL LEARN: IMITATION**

This Little Toe

◆ Rub each of the baby's toes gently as you recite this rhyme.

> *This little toe goes a rub-a-dub-dub.*
> *This little toe goes a scrub-a-scrub-scrub.*
> *Rub-a-dub-dub,*
> *Scrub-a-scrub-scrub,*
> *This little toe goes*
> *SPLASH!*

◆ Change your voice when you say, "SPLASH!"

◆ Each time you play this game, change the way you say, "SPLASH!" Speak in a high voice, a low voice, a soft voice, a whisper. I'm sure you will have ideas of your own.

◆ WHAT YOUR BABY WILL LEARN:
FUN

How Does It Feel?

◆ Punch two finger holes in a narrow box.

◆ Line the box with materials of different textures—fur, burlap, velvet, sandpaper. Tape the box closed.

◆ Show the baby how to poke a finger through a hole. Poke your finger into the other hole.

◆ Talk to the baby about how the materials feel. Are they soft, rough, bumpy?

◆ This is a good game for the car.

◆ WHAT YOUR BABY WILL LEARN:
ABOUT TEXTURES

Where's the Sound?

◆ Give the baby a rattle and help him shake it. See whether he can shake it by himself.

◆ Place the rattle in his other hand. Help him shake it, then see if he can shake it by himself.

◆ Watch to see whether his eyes focus on the source of the sound.

◆ Shake the rattle while saying, "Shake, shake, rattle, shake."

◆ Give the baby the rattle and repeat those words as he shakes the rattle.

◆ Continue this game to help your baby realize that his hand is doing the shaking.

  WHAT YOUR BABY WILL LEARN:
ABOUT SOUNDS

Little Train

◆ Move your fingers up and down along your baby's arm as you recite this rhyme.

> *This little train ran up the track,*
> *Toot, toot, toot.*
> *This little train ran up the track*
> *And then it came toot-tooting back,*
> *Toot, Toot. (Make your voice sound like a*
> *train whistle)*

◆ Repeat the rhyme, moving your baby's fingers up and down along your arm.

◆ Be sure to say, "toot, toot" at the end.

WHAT YOUR BABY WILL LEARN:
LANGUAGE SKILLS

MONTHS

Swim Little Fishie

◆ This game is fun to do in the bathtub or a swimming pool.

◆ Recite the rhyme while moving your hand under the water like a fish

> *Swim little fishie,*
> *Swim around the pool.*
> *Swim little fishie,*
> *The water is cool.*
> *Where's the little fishie?*
> *Where did he go?*
> *There he is!*
> *SPLASH, SPLASH!*

◆ Gently splash your baby as you say, "SPLASH, SPLASH!"

◆ **WHAT YOUR BABY WILL LEARN: LANGUAGE SKILLS**

Finger and Toe Games 193

Five Little Fingers

◆ Hold your baby's fingers in your hand. Move one finger back and forth, saying, "wiggle little finger."

◆ Do this with each finger.

◆ Repeat the same steps, wiggling the baby's toes.

◆ Recite this rhyme to the baby as you wiggle her fingers or toes.

> *What can I do with five little fingers?*
> *What can I do with five little fingers?*
> *What can I do with five little fingers?*
> *What can I do today?*
>
> *I can wiggle my five little fingers.*
> *I can wiggle my five little fingers.*
> *I can wiggle my five little fingers.*
> *I can wiggle them today.*

◆ Also try shaking five little fingers (or waving, clapping, and so on).

WHAT YOUR BABY WILL LEARN:
BODY AWARENESS

Touch Your Fingers

◆ Cradle your baby's hand in yours and gently stroke each finger, saying, "finger."

◆ Gently stroke each toe, saying, "toe."

◆ Place your baby's fingers on his toes.

◆ Sing to the tune of "Mary Had A Little Lamb."

> *Touch your fingers to your toes,*
> *To your toes, to your toes.*
> *Touch your fingers to your toes,*
> *One, two, three, four, five.*

◆ Touch each finger or toe as you say the numbers.

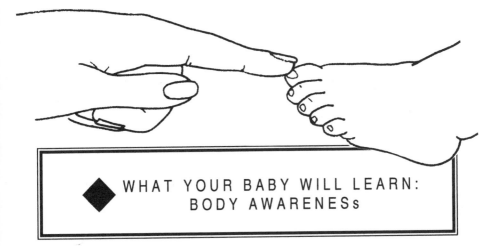

WHAT YOUR BABY WILL LEARN:
BODY AWARENESs

The Dropping Game

◆ You will need a small ball and an empty coffee can for this game. **NOTE**: Be sure that the coffee can has no sharp edges.

◆ Sit the baby on the floor and set the coffee can in front of her.

◆ Place the ball in the baby's hand and hold it over the can. Open her fingers to let the ball drop into the can.

◆ When you hear the ball strike the can, say, "boom."

◆ Repeat this several times, and soon the baby will drop the ball all by herself.

◆ The baby may need help retrieving the ball.

WHAT YOUR BABY WILL LEARN:
TO DROP OBJECTS

Touch This

◆ Find a quiet time when you and your baby can play together without interruption.

◆ Collect items that have a variety of textures, for example, foil, cotton balls, emery boards, corduroy, velvet, satin, wool, waxed paper and cork.

◆ Glue several items onto a large piece of cardboard.

◆ Place the baby's hand on each item and tell him what he is touching. Make comments like "smooth," "nice," "soft" and "cool."

◆ This game is also excellent for language development.

◆ WHAT YOUR BABY WILL LEARN:
ABOUT TEXTURES

Piggy, Piggy

◆ Word games that involve the baby's fingers and toes will delight your infant and create a special bond between the two of you.

◆ Recite this rhyme to your baby while playing with her feet.

> *Piggy, piggy, where are you?*
>   *(Wiggle baby's big toe)*
> *Piggy, piggy, where's your shoe?*
>   *(Shake baby's foot)*
> *Piggy, piggy, googie goo,*
>   *(Kiss baby's toe)*
> *I love my little piggy.*
>   *(Pick up baby and cuddle him)*

WHAT YOUR BABY WILL LEARN:
BONDING

Pinkety Pinkety

◆ Recite this rhyme while playing with the baby's thumbs.

Pinkety, pinkety, thumb to thumb,
Wish a wish, and it's sure to come.
   (Put your thumbs on the baby's thumbs)
If yours come true, mine will come true,
   (Wrap your thumbs around the baby's thumbs)
Pinkety, pinkety, thumb to thumb.
   (Kiss baby's thumbs)

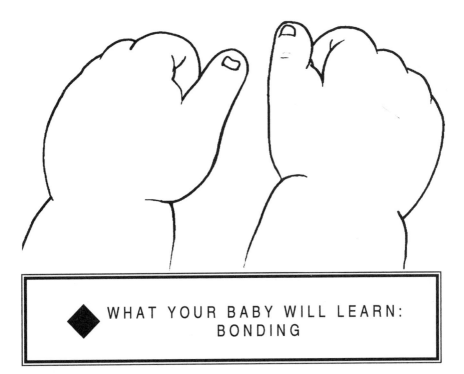

◆ WHAT YOUR BABY WILL LEARN:
BONDING

Pat My Baby's Toe

◆ Touching your baby and saying loving words to her will develop trust and bonding.

◆ Sing this song to the tune of "London Bridge Is Falling Down."

> *Pat my little baby's toe,*
> *Pat, pat, pat,*
> *Pat, pat, pat.*
> *Pat my little baby's toe,*
> *Kiss the baby.*

◆ When you sing the word "pat," gently tap the baby's toe. When you sing the word "kiss," hold your baby close and kiss her.

WHAT YOUR BABY WILL LEARN:
BONDING

MONTHS

Rub Rub Toe Toe

◆ Gently rub one toe at a time as you sing to the tune of "Twinkle, Twinkle, Little Star."

Rub, rub, toe, toe, rub, rub, toe.
Rub, rub, toe, toe, rub, rub, toe.

◆ Repeat until you have massaged each toe.

◆ Repeat the same game, rubbing one finger at a time.

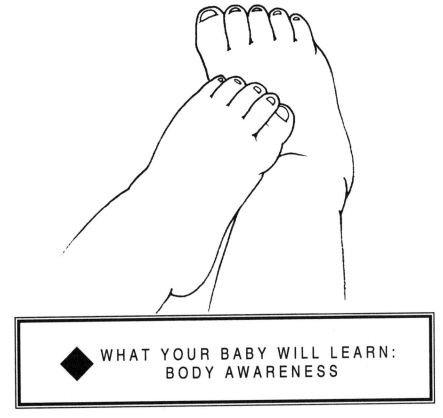

◆ WHAT YOUR BABY WILL LEARN:
BODY AWARENESS

Creeping

◆ Creep your fingers up the baby's arm as you recite this rhyme.

> *Creeping, creeping, creeping*
> *Comes the little cat.*
> *Meow, meow, meow, meow,*
> *Meow, meow, meow, meow,*
> *Just like that.*

◆ Repeat the poem using another animal and its characteristic sound.

> *Creeping, creeping, creeping*
> *Comes the little dog.*
> *Woof, woof...etc.*

◆ Encourage your child to make the animal's sound.

◆ WHAT YOUR BABY WILL LEARN:
ABOUT ANIMAL SOUNDS

The Cracker Game

◆ Take a bite out of a cracker. Give your baby a bite.

◆ Break the cracker into small pieces and pick up one piece to eat. Encourage your baby to do the same.

◆ Drop a piece of cracker into a film canister. Turn it upside down and shake out the cracker.

◆ Again drop a piece of cracker into the film canister, and see if your baby can shake it out.

◆ Place several pieces into the canister. This time snap on the lid. Let your baby try taking off the lid to retrieve the crackers.

◆ WHAT YOUR BABY WILL LEARN:
TO PICK UP SMALL OBJECTS

The Pettitoes

♦ This traditional English rhyme goes back generations.

♦ Recite the rhyme while following the directions.

> *The pettitoes are little feet,*
> > *(Kiss the baby's feet and move them in a circle)*
> *And the little feet not big.*
> *Great feet belong to the grunting hog,*
> > *(Grunt like a pig)*
> *And the pettitoes to the little pig.*
> > *(Tickle the baby's toes and say "wee wee" as you touch each of them.)*

WHAT YOUR BABY WILL LEARN:
FUN

In the Barn

◆ Games like "In the Barn" teach babies trust and help them develop a sense of humor.

◆ Recite the rhyme while following the directions.

> *The bumblebee went in the barn,*
>> *(Gently poke your index finger into your baby's tummy)*
>
> *Carrying dinner under his arm.*
>> *(Gently poke baby under the arm)*
>
> *Buzzzzzzz-z-z-z!*
>> *(Tickle your baby all over with your fingers)*

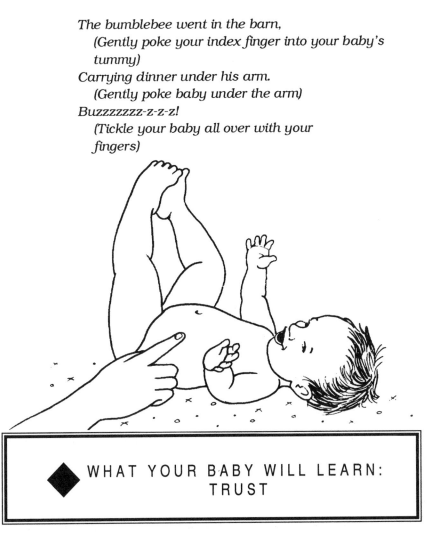

◆ **WHAT YOUR BABY WILL LEARN: TRUST**

Open, Shut Them

(Be prepared for lots of laughter)

◆ Your baby will love the surprise ending.

◆ Recite the poem and act out the words with your fingers as the baby watches.

> *Open, shut them,*
> *Open, shut them,*
> *Give a little clap.*
> *Open, shut them,*
> *Open, shut them,*
> *Put them in your lap.*
>
> *Creep them, creep them,*
> *Creep them, creep them,*
> *Right up to your chin.*
> *Open up*
> *Your little mouth,*
> *But do not let them in.*

◆ Start at your waist when you creep to your chin.

◆ Slow the pace on "Open up your little mouth." Wait a second, then say very quickly, "But do not let them in," and hide your hands behind your back.

◆ The baby will soon try to imitate your actions.

WHAT YOUR BABY WILL LEARN:
IMITATION

Water and Spoon

◆ Your baby will be fascinated with this game.

◆ Place a fairly shallow plastic bowl and a large spoon on a table in front of your baby.

◆ Fill the bowl with water.

◆ Next to the bowl, put an empty cup. Show the baby how to dip the spoon into the water and fill up the cup.

◆ Adding some pieces of ice makes for even more fun.

◆ WHAT YOUR BABY WILL LEARN:
TO USE A SPOON

Bedtime for Piggies

◆ This is a toe counting game that your baby will love.

◆ Recite the rhyme to your baby.

> *"It's time for piggies to go to bed,"*
> *Mother Piggie said.*
> *"I will count them up to see,*
> *If all of my piggies came back to me."*
>
> *"One little piggie, two little piggies,*
> *Three little piggies, dear.*
> *Four little piggies, five little piggies,*
> *Yes, they all are here.*
> *You are the dearest piggies alive,*
> *One, two, three, four, five."*

◆ Start counting your baby's toes as you begin the second verse.

WHAT YOUR BABY WILL LEARN:
FUN

Baby Mice

◆ Your baby will be delighted as this story unfolds.

◆ Recite the rhyme, following the directions.

Where are the baby mice?
Squeak, squeak, squeak.
  (Speak in a squeaky voice and hide your hand
  behind your back)
I cannot see them,
Peek, peek, peek.
  (Bring your fist forward where the baby can see it)
Here they come
  (Speak with anticipation)
Out of the hole,
One, two, three, four, five
  (Open your fist and raise one finger at a time)
And that is all.

◆ WHAT YOUR BABY WILL LEARN:
FUN

The Snail

◆ Cup one hand. While reciting the poem, creep the fingers of the other hand into the cupped one.

> *Hand in hand you see us well,*
> *Creep like a snail into his shell.*
> *Ever nearer, ever nearer,*
> *Ever closer, ever closer,*
> *Very snug indeed you dwell,*
> *Snail within your tiny shell.*

◆ Cup your hand and let your baby creep her fingers into it.

◆ Show the baby how to cup her hand. Creep your fingers into it.

◆ WHAT YOUR BABY WILL LEARN: FUN

The Glove Game

◆ Sit on the floor with your baby.

◆ Put a garden glove on your hand. Wiggle your fingers inside the glove.

◆ Put the garden glove on your baby's hand and wiggle the baby's fingers. When you wiggle his fingers, say silly words like "wiggle, wiggle."

◆ Remove the glove from the baby's hand and see whether he can put it back on by himself. This will probably take time. If he gets frustrated, help and encourage him.

◆ Play a "glove talk" game with your baby. Put a glove on your baby's hand and one on your hand. Move the glove on your hand and see if he will move the glove on his hand.

◆ Try putting the glove on the baby's foot.

◆ Try putting the glove on a doll's hand or foot.

 WHAT YOUR BABY WILL LEARN:
PROBLEM-SOLVING SKILLS

This Little Cow

◆ Play this game with either fingers or toes. Grasp one of your baby's fingers or toes at a time as you describe each cow.

> This little cow eats grass,
> This little cow eats hay,
> This little cow looks over the bridge,
> This little cow runs away.
> And this little cow does nothing at all,
> But lie in the fields all day.
>
> Let's chase this little cow.
> Chase, chase, chase, chase, chase.

◆ On the last line, tickle your baby all over.

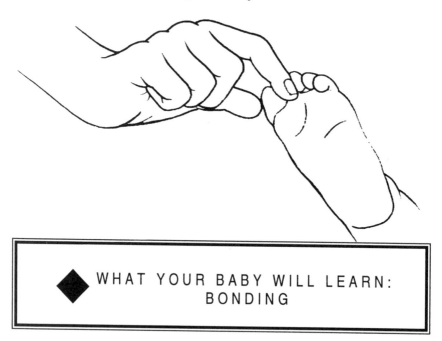

◆ **WHAT YOUR BABY WILL LEARN:**
BONDING

If You're Happy

◆ Help your baby learn the many ways she can move her fingers and toes.

◆ Sing to the tune of "If You're Happy and You Know It."

> *If you're happy and you know it, wiggle your fingers.*
> *If you're happy and you know it, wiggle your fingers.*
> *If you're happy and you know it,*
> *Then your smile (big smile) will surely show it.*
> *If you're happy and you know it, wiggle your fingers.*

◆ Make up new verses and sing to show your baby what she can do with her fingers and toes.

Wiggle toes....
Shake fingers and toes....
Open and close....
Move in a circle....
Tickle....

 WHAT YOUR BABY WILL LEARN:
BODY AWARENESS

Through the Hole

◆ Put your thumb and index finger together to make a circle.

◆ Point one finger on your other hand and put it through the circle.Say "BOO!"

◆ Recite the rhyme, wiggling your finger.

> *Wiggle your finger, one and two,*
> *Wiggle your finger, one and two,*
> *Wiggle your finger, one and two,*
> *Through the hole and BOO!!*

◆ On "BOO!" point your finger through the circle and shake it.

◆ Now let your baby play the game and push his finger through the circle. When you say, "BOO," kiss the baby's finger.

◆ Try to teach your baby how to make the circle with his thumb and finger. Put your finger through the circle.

◆ WHAT YOUR BABY WILL LEARN:
COORDINATION

This Is the Father

◆ Wiggle one of your baby's fingers at a time, starting with the thumb, as you recite.

> *This is the father, short and stout.*
> *This is the mother with children about.*
> *This is the brother, tall you see.*
> *This is the sister with doll on her knee.*
> *This is the baby sure to grow.*
> *And here is the family, all in a row.*

◆ On the last line, hold up all five fingers and shake them.

◆ Play the game again, wiggling one toe at a time, starting with the big toe.

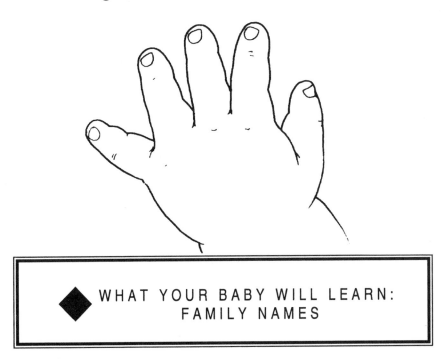

◆ WHAT YOUR BABY WILL LEARN: FAMILY NAMES

Bath and Dressing
Games

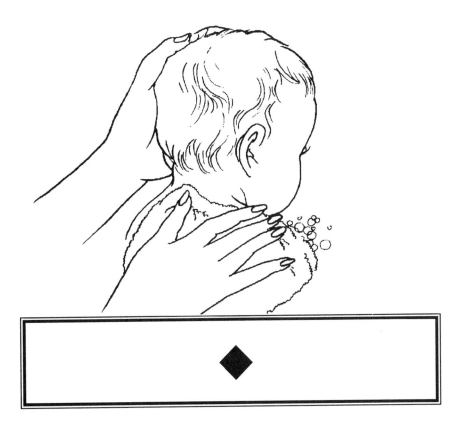

Hold It Tight

◆ Hold a small toy in front of your baby where he can see it.

◆ Touch the inside of his hand with the toy and help him close his fingers around it.

◆ Take your hand away, leaving him holding the toy.

◆ When he drops the toy, give it to him again and speak in loving tones.

◆ As you play this game, the baby's fingers will grow stronger, and soon he will be able to open and close his hands voluntarily.

◆ Each time, return the toy to the baby's opposite hand.

◆ For tactile experiences, alternate toys that are soft, hard, cool, smooth, etc.

WHAT YOUR BABY WILL LEARN: TO HOLD OBJECTS

The Hand Discovery

◆ Around three months, babies experience an exciting event—they discover their hands.

◆ This game will help the process along and give your baby endless pleasure.

◆ Lay the baby on her back and talk softly to her so that you have her complete attention.

◆ Place her hand gently on her cheek. As you are doing this, say, "Baby's hand is so nice."

◆ After a few times, hold her hand in front of her eyes before and after you put it on her cheek.

◆ The baby learns to associate pleasure with seeing her hands.

WHAT YOUR BABY WILL LEARN:
BODY AWARENESS

Loving Kisses

◆ When you dress the baby or change a diaper, this game is lovely to play.

◆ Say, "I love your nose, nose, nose, nose." Kiss the baby on his nose.

◆ Say, "I love your tummy, tummy, tummy, tummy." Kiss the baby on his tummy.

◆ Repeat, naming other parts of the body and kissing the baby.

◆ This game helps the baby become aware of his body and of the love that you express.

◆ WHAT YOUR BABY WILL LEARN:
BODY AWARENESS

Baby's Bath

◆ For a relaxing change of pace, take a warm bath with your baby.

◆ Hold the baby as you rock back and forth.

◆ Sing to the baby as you rock. Make up songs like, "We are taking a bath together," "I love my little baby, baby, baby," and so on.

◆ The song is not important, but the bonding is.

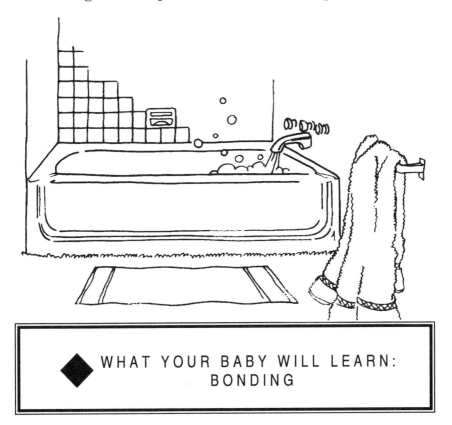

◆ WHAT YOUR BABY WILL LEARN:
BONDING

Sweet Baby Mine

◆ Play this game anytime that you dress your baby. It's especially nice after a bath.

◆ Massage and stroke the baby.

◆ Tell the baby that you love her. Talk about the parts of her body that you are massaging.

◆ Recite this poem as you dress the baby.

> *(Mama or Daddy) loves you so, sweet baby mine.*
> *You are so soft and nice to touch.*
> *I'll wiggle your nose and ten of your toes,*
> *Then go 'round and 'round on your nice soft tummy.*
> *Now for a kiss, sweet baby mine.*
> *You are so soft and nice to cuddle.*

◆ **WHAT YOUR BABY WILL LEARN:**
BONDING

MONTHS

Follow the Toy

(This game is excellent for developing eye coordination)

◆ Attract the baby's attention by shaking a rattle approximately one foot from his face.

◆ When the baby fixes his eyes on the rattle, slowly move it in a half circle.

◆ Now try the same thing with a speaking toy. By changing the object, you will hold the infant's attention for a longer period.

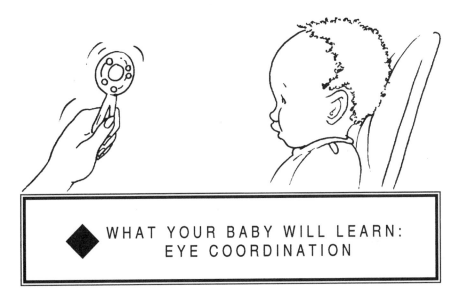

◆ WHAT YOUR BABY WILL LEARN:
EYE COORDINATION

Where's the Rattle?

◆ While the baby is lying on her back, shake a rattle, first on one side of her head, and then on the other.

◆ When the baby begins to search for the sound—you can tell by watching his eyes—turn her head toward the sound.

◆ Place the rattle in the baby's hand. Move her hand back and forth and watch her look for the noise.

◆ Say encouraging things to the baby as she searches for the sound. The encouragement from your voice will help her keep trying and succeed.

◆ Phrases to say include, "You're doing well," "I'm proud of you."

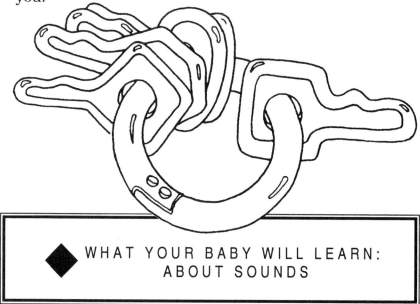

◆ WHAT YOUR BABY WILL LEARN:
ABOUT SOUNDS

Can You Find Me?

- This game is good practice for coordinating sound and sight.

- While the baby is lying in the crib, go to another part of the room and call his name.

- Go back to the crib and say his name as you stroke his head.

- Go to another part of the room and say the baby's name.

- Then return to the crib and repeat his name as you stroke his head.

- As you continue to say his name in different parts of the room, the baby will move his eyes in search of the sound. By returning to the crib each time, you ensure he hears the sound close by as well as far away.

 WHAT YOUR BABY WILL LEARN:
ABOUT SOUNDS

Motor Boat

◆ This is a popular game to play while changing a diaper.

◆ While the baby is lying on her back, take hold of one foot in each of your hands.

◆ Start moving her legs back and forth, slowly and then faster, as you repeat the following rhyme.

> *Motorboat, motorboat, go so slow,*
> *Motorboat, motorboat, step on the gas,*
> *Motorboat, motorboat, go so fast.*

◆ WHAT YOUR BABY WILL LEARN:
FUN

Washing Baby

◆ Bath time is a wonderful time to develop your baby's self-concept. As you wash the baby, sing about the different parts of the body.

◆ Sing to the tune of "London Bridge is Falling Down."

> *Head and shoulders, knees and toes,*
> *Knees and toes, knees and toes.*
> *Head and shoulders, knees and toes,*
> *Eyes and ears and mouth and nose.*

◆ Wash each part of the body as you are sing about it.

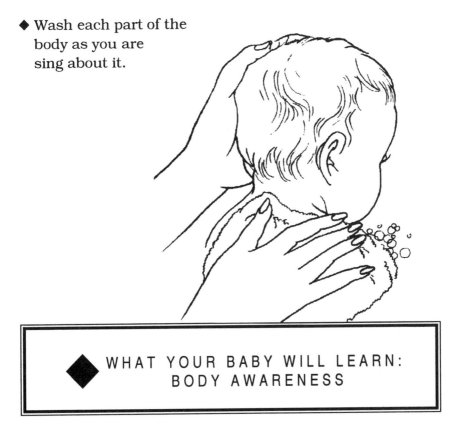

◆ WHAT YOUR BABY WILL LEARN:
BODY AWARENESS

Baby's Fingers

◆ This game develops body awareness and vocabulary. It also provides a wonderful opportunity to bond with your baby.

◆ While you dress your baby, you have the perfect opportunity to talk about different parts of the body.

◆ Gently touch each of the baby's fingers. As you do so, say in a singsong voice, "This is (child's name)'s finger."

◆ Place the baby's hand on your finger. In the same voice, say, "This is (Mommy/Daddy/Grandma's) finger."

WHAT YOUR BABY WILL LEARN:
BODY AWARENESS

Hello, Hands

◆ At this age, when babies like to explore their hands and feet, they enjoy this game.

◆ Take a pair of your baby's socks and cut five holes in each for fingers.

◆ Decorate the socks with bright colors and interesting shapes or faces.

◆ Fit the socks on baby's hands for him to look at, talk to and enjoy.

◆ Remember to choose decorations cautiously because the baby will most likely put his hands in his mouth.

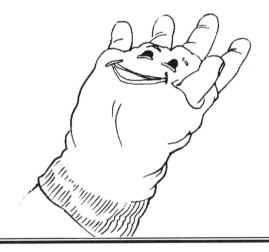

◆ WHAT YOUR BABY WILL LEARN:
ABOUT COLORS

Diaper Fun

◆ Games like this one develop a child's sense of humor.

◆ Make diaper changing a fun time. Hold the diaper in front of your face, then take it away and say, "peek-a-boo."

◆ Hold the diaper in front of your face, bend your head down next to the baby's head and say, "peek-a-boo" in a soft voice.

◆ Wave the diaper back and forth in front of your face and say, "peek-a-boo."

◆ WHAT YOUR BABY WILL LEARN:
A SENSE OF HUMOR

Massage Time

◆ Games like this create a very special bond between parent and child.

◆ After a bath give your baby a nice massage.

◆ Take your hands and gently massage the baby's body while you say loving words to her.

◆ If your baby has no allergy problems, use baby powder to massage her.

◆ As you massage the baby, name the parts of the body that you touch. For example, "You have such a pretty foot. Now I'll massage your foot."

◆ Turn your baby on her tummy and massage her back, the back of her legs, heels, etc.

 WHAT YOUR BABY WILL LEARN: BONDING

Charlie Chaplin

◆ Lay the baby on her back.

◆ Recite this poem to your baby while moving her legs as directed.

> *Charlie Chaplin went to France*
> *To teach the ladies how to dance.*
> *First he did the rhumba,*
>   *(Move the baby's knees back and forth)*
> *Then he did the kicks,*
>   *(Move the baby's legs in a kicking motion)*
> *Then he did the samba,*
>   *(Put the baby's legs together and move*
>   *them up and down)*
> *Then he did the splits.*
>   *(Gently move the baby's legs apart*
>   *and then back together)*

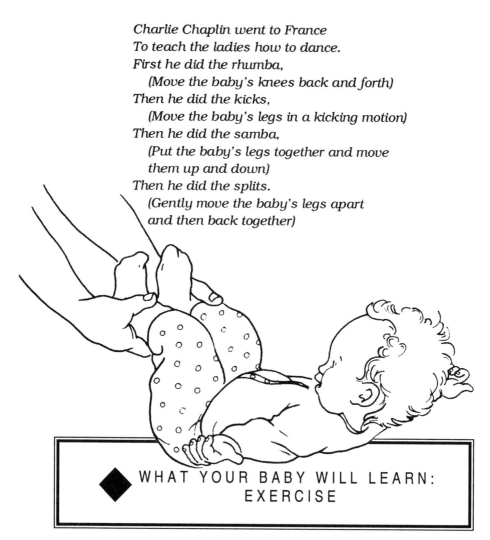

◆ WHAT YOUR BABY WILL LEARN:
EXERCISE

One, Two, Kick!

◆ Lie on the floor next to your baby.

◆ Put a small blanket over your feet, then kick it off.

◆ When you kick off the blanket, recite this poem.

> *One, two, kick it off, kick it off,*
> *Kick it off.*
> *One, two, kick it off,*
> *Kick it off my darling.*

◆ This poem may also be sung to the tune of "Skip To My Lou."

◆ Lay the baby on the floor and the blanket over her feet. Sing the song and help her kick off the blanket.

◆ WHAT YOUR BABY WILL LEARN: EXERCISE

Ball Rolls

♦ A large beach ball can be a wonderful tool for exercising your baby and having fun as well.

♦ Put your baby on his tummy on top of a beach ball.

♦ Hold the baby firmly, rolling the ball back and forth.
   NOTE: Always hold the baby while he is on top of the ball.

♦ Recite this poem as you roll the ball.

> *Roll the ball, roll the ball,*
> *Back and forth, back and forth,*
> *Roll the ball, roll the ball,*
> *One, two, whooooo!*

♦ On the word "whoooo!" kiss the baby on his back.

◆ WHAT YOUR BABY WILL LEARN:
EXERCISE

Bend and Stretch

◆ Lay your baby on her back on a flat, padded surface. Hold her feet and gently raise them near her face saying, "Bend and stretch, bend and stretch."

◆ Gently touch the baby's right foot to her nose. Gently touch her left foot to her nose. Each time, say, "Bend and stretch, bend and stretch."

◆ Cross the baby's arms in and out over her chest, saying, "Bend and stretch, bend and stretch."

◆ Let the baby grasp your index fingers. Raise her arms up and down while saying, "Bend and stretch, bend and stretch."

◆ Finally, holding the baby's hands, lift her to a sitting position, then release her gently back down, saying, "Bend and stretch, bend and stretch."

◆ Eventually the baby will pull up to a standing position and love every minute of this exercise.

WHAT YOUR BABY WILL LEARN:
EXERCISE

Backstroke Baby

◆ This game usually delights babies.

◆ Fill the baby's bath with a very small amount of water—
maybe one-third full.

◆ Lay the baby on his back and let him kick.

◆ Keep your hand on the baby's head so that he won't get
any water in his ears.

◆ While the baby kicks his legs, sing to the tune of "Row,
Row, Row Your Boat."

Kick, kick, kick your legs,
Kick them all the time.
Merrily, merrily, merrily, merrily,
Kick them all the time.

◆ **WHAT YOUR BABY WILL LEARN:
EXERCISE**

Who Do You See?

◆ Changing diapers is a wonderful opportunity to share special time with your baby and help him in his development.

◆ Put pictures on walls near the changing table so that he can look at them while you change him.

◆ Start with pictures of family members. As he looks at them, ask him, "Who do you see?"

◆ Always name the person after you ask him who he sees.

◆ Tack up pictures of animals and ask the child the name of the animal and what sound it makes.

WHAT YOUR BABY WILL LEARN:
LANGUAGE SKILLS

Wash Those Toes

♦ Sing this song to your baby as you bathe her.

♦ Sing to the tune of "Here We Go Round the Mulberry Bush."

> *This is the way we wash our toes,*
> *Wash our toes, wash our toes.*
> *This is the way we wash our toes,*
> *I love you.*

♦ Repeat the song, singing about a different part of the body. "This is the way we wash our hands," "This is the way we wash our nose," and so on.

♦ After you have sung the song a few times, ask the baby: "Where's your toe?" "Where's your nose?"

WHAT YOUR BABY WILL LEARN:
BODY AWARENESS

Zip, Zip, Zip

◆ Diapering a baby gets harder as he gets older. Reciting a special poem will keep the baby's attention.

> *Zip, zip, zip, off it goes!*
> *I see baby without clothes.*
> *Zip, zip, what do I see?*
> *Diaper on, one, two, three!*

◆ Trying to say "zip" is great fun for the baby.

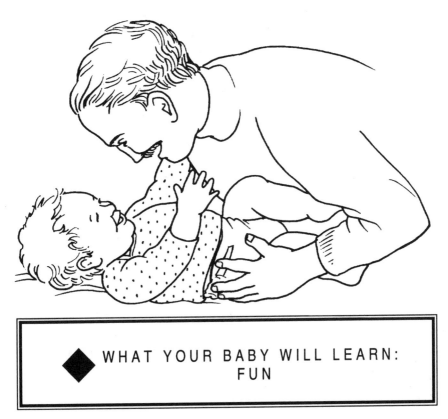

WHAT YOUR BABY WILL LEARN:
FUN

Rub-a-Dub-Dub

◆ Recite this familiar nursery rhyme to your baby while he is in the bath.

> *Rub-a-dub-dub,*
> *Three men in a tub.*
> *And who do you think they be?*
> *The butcher, the baker,*
> *The candlestick maker,*
> *And little babies three.*

◆ As you say the rhyme, move your baby back and forth in the water. A gentle gliding motion is very soothing to a baby. On the words "little babies three," turn the baby around or lift him out of the water.

◆ If you are teaching your baby to swim, this is a wonderful game to play at the swimming pool.

WHAT YOUR BABY WILL LEARN:
FUN

Ten Little Toesies

◆ In or out of the bath, your baby will enjoy this song.

◆ As you sing, gently touch each toe or finger. When you come to the last line, splash the water or turn the baby around in the water.

◆ While you dry the baby, pat each toe or finger. At the end, do something different. A nice big hug is fun! Sing the song to the tune of "Ten Little Indians."

One little, two little, three little toesies,
Four little, five little, six little toesies,
Seven little, eight little, nine little toesies,
Ten little tickle toes.

Ten little, nine little, eight little toesies,
Seven little, six little, five little toesies,
Four little, three little, two little toesies,
One little tickle toe.

◆ WHAT YOUR BABY WILL LEARN:
COUNTING SKILLS

Shoe Game

◆ This is a poem for putting on the baby's shoes.

> *Shoe the old horse.*
> *Shoe the old mare.*
> *But let the little colt*
> *Go bare, bare, bare.*

◆ Recite the last line as the baby's shoe is tied, tapping the sole of the foot each time you say, "bare, bare, bare."

◆ The baby will begin to look forward to the tapping.

◆ WHAT YOUR BABY WILL LEARN:
FUN

The Rainmaker

◆ Play this rainmaking game in the bathtub.

◆ Punch holes in a plastic bottle and give it to your baby.

◆ Show her how to fill the bottle with water and hold it in the air to make it rain.

◆ Your baby will delight in this activity. While you play, here are two "rain" songs to sing.

Rain, rain, go away,
Come again another day.
Little (child's name) wants to play.

It's raining, it's pouring,
The old man is snoring.
Went to bed, that sleepy head,
Won't get up until morning.

 WHAT YOUR BABY WILL LEARN:
FUN

So-o-o Big

◆ Play this game while the baby is lying on her back on a flat surface.

◆ Reach out to grasp your baby's fingers. Gently raise the baby to a sitting position and say, "(*Baby's name*) is so-o-o big!"

◆ If the baby cannot hold onto your hands, place them over her fingers.

◆ As the baby grows older, say, "Up so-o-o high and down we go," as you gently raise the baby up and then let her down.

◆ WHAT YOUR BABY WILL LEARN:
TO SIT UP

The Kiss, Kiss Song

◆ Sit in a chair and hold your baby upright with his feet over your knees.

◆ Bounce the baby on your knees and sing to the tune of "Ten Little Indian."

> *One little, two little, three little kiss, kiss.*
>   *(Bounce baby on your knees)*
> *Four little, five little, six little kiss, kiss.*
>   *(Bounce baby on your upper thighs)*
> *Seven little, eight little, nine little kiss, kiss*
>   *(Bounce baby on your tummy)*
> *Ten little kisses, I love you.*
>   *(Hold the baby close and give him a big hug)*

◆ Repeat the game backwards.

WHAT YOUR BABY WILL LEARN:
BONDING

Mirror Parts

◆ Hold your baby in front of a mirror.

◆ While she is looking in the mirror, touch her nose and say, "Here's your nose."

◆ Touch her head and say, "Here's your head."

◆ Ask the baby to touch her nose. Then ask here to touch her head.

◆ Touch your nose and say, "Here's my nose." Repeat with your head.

◆ Ask the baby to touch your nose and head.

◆ WHAT YOUR BABY WILL LEARN:
BODY AWARENESS

Powder Puff Fun

◆ This is a great way to keep your baby still while you change his diaper.

◆ Give a large powder puff to your baby. Let him feel and explore it.

◆ Rub the powder puff on his tummy and recite this rhyme.

Powder puff, powder puff,
On your tummy, on your tummy.
Powder puff, powder puff,
Tummy, tummy, boo!

◆ Tickle your baby on the word "boo!"

◆ Continue placing the puff on different parts of his body. Each time you touch a new part, name that part in the poem.

 WHAT YOUR BABY WILL LEARN:
BODY AWARENESS

The Washing Game

◆ This game is best played at bath time. Give your baby her own tightly wrung out washcloth.

◆ Make up your own melody and sing the words, "Can you wash your face?" Take the baby's hand and rub the washcloth gently on her face, then sing, "Yes, I can, yes, I can."

◆ Continue playing this game as you name all parts of the body: hands, feet, cheek, nose, ears, and so on.

◆ Next ask the baby to wash your face, your hands, your nose, etc.

◆ To dry the baby, play the same game by giving the baby a towel with which to dry herself.

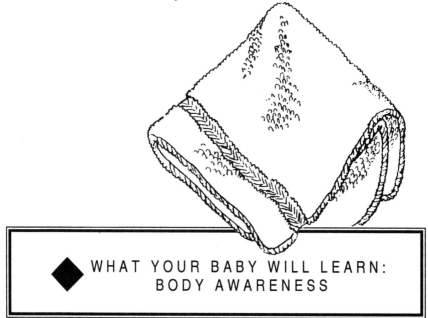

◆ WHAT YOUR BABY WILL LEARN:
BODY AWARENESS

A Bath Surprise

◆ While your baby is in the bathtub, show her a floating toy. Let her hold it for a few minutes.

◆ Take the toy from your baby and place it in the water in front of her.

◆ Cover the toy with a washcloth and ask, "Where is the toy? Where did it go?"

◆ Remove the washcloth and say, "Hooray, here it is. It was hiding under the washcloth."

◆ Play this game several times and encourage the baby to lift the washcloth off the toy.

◆ If the baby doesn't understand after the first few times, you can guide her hands to remove the washcloth.

 WHAT YOUR BABY WILL LEARN:
COGNITIVE SKILLS

Squeeze Fun

◆ This is a lovely game to play at bath time.

◆ Fill the bathtub with several squeeze toys, sponges and a washcloth.

◆ Ask the baby to squeeze one of the toys. Ask him if you may have a turn.

◆ When you have squeezed two or three toys, take a sponge and squeeze it on your hand.

◆ Ask the baby if you may squeeze it on his hand.

◆ Repeat this with the washcloth. First squeeze it on your hand, then his.

◆ Now show the baby how to squeeze the sponge or wash-cloth on one of the toys.

◆ WHAT YOUR BABY WILL LEARN:
TO STRENGTHEN HAND MUSCLES

Floating Surprise

◆ Wrap a bath toy that will float in a washcloth. Move it around the bathtub.

◆ Give it to your baby and see whether she can unwrap it.

◆ After the toy is unwrapped, squeeze the water from the washcloth over it.

◆ Ask your baby to squeeze the cloth over the toy.

◆ As the water is dripping, shout "Whee!"

◆ Ask the baby to wrap the toy for you. This requires great skill of your child.

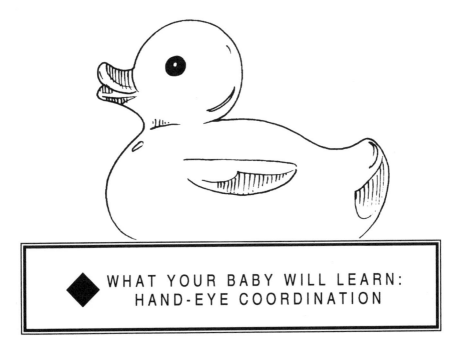

◆ WHAT YOUR BABY WILL LEARN:
HAND-EYE COORDINATION

Catch the Toy

- ◆ Babies love to play in water. Pouring skills can be practiced in or out of the tub.

- ◆ Show your baby how to scoop and pour water with a ladle into a container.

- ◆ Give the baby a strainer to scoop the water and let her experience the difference between the strainer and the ladle.

- ◆ Place floating toys in the bathtub. Let the baby try to catch the toys in the ladle and in the strainer.

- ◆ In addition to developing hand-eye coordination, this activity also teaches about volume.

 WHAT YOUR BABY WILL LEARN: HAND-EYE COORDINATION

Going to Sleep Games

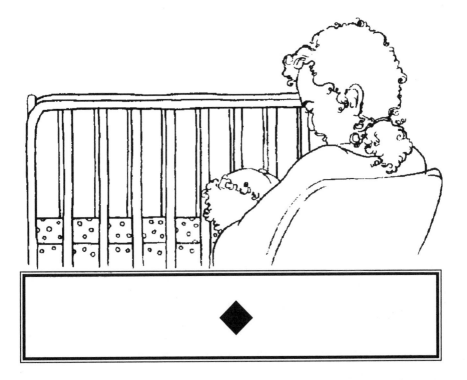

Good Night, Baby

◆ While your baby is feeding, gently massage her fingers and toes.

◆ Softly sing to her as she is feeding, to the tune of "Twinkle, Twinkle, Little Star."

> *Good night, baby, I love you.*
> *(Or use your child's name)*
> *I will take good care of you.*

◆ Keep repeating this song as you massage the baby's fingers and toes.

◆ This game will help the baby associate feeding with your loving touch.

◆ Singing to babies while they are feeding is pleasureful for both you and your baby.

◆ **WHAT YOUR BABY WILL LEARN:**
BONDING

Good Night Kisses

◆ Rock your baby gently in your arms.

◆ The light in the room should be soft and muted.

◆ Kiss the baby on the forehead and say:

> *I love you, I love you,*
> *I love my little (child's name).*

◆ Kiss the baby on his fingers and repeat the words.

◆ Continue kissing the baby on different parts of his body, repeating the words.

◆ WHAT YOUR BABY WILL LEARN:
BONDING

Rock-a-Bye Baby

◆ Hold your baby in your arms and sing this familiar lullaby.

Rock-a-bye baby,
On the tree top,
When the wind blows,
The cradle will rock.
When the bough breaks,
The cradle will fall,
And down will come baby,
Cradle and all.

Rock-a-bye baby,
Thy cradle is green,
Daddy's a nobleman,
Mommy's a queen.
Betty's a lady,
And wears a gold ring,
Johnny's a drummer
And drums for the king.

◆ WHAT YOUR BABY WILL LEARN:
A BEDTIME ROUTINE

Bedtime Talk

◆ The more you talk to your baby, the sooner she will babble and try to talk.

◆ When it's bedtime, a soothing voice and loving words can help him fall asleep more easily.

◆ Say things like "Good night, sweet baby," or "Rest, rest, rest your little head."

◆ Hold the baby close to you and stroke his face or head as you talk to him.

◆ As you put him in the crib, continue to say comfort- ing words and caress the baby.

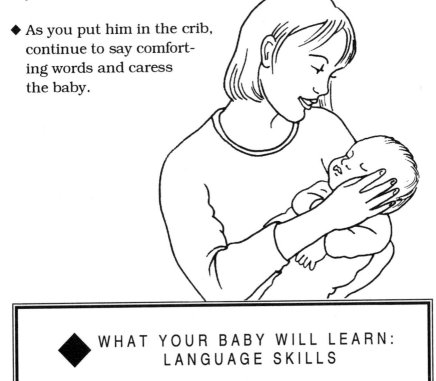

◆ WHAT YOUR BABY WILL LEARN:
LANGUAGE SKILLS

Sleepy Time

◆ Caring for babies tenderly makes them feel loved and accepted.

◆ Singing lullabies while swaying with the baby in your arms is a wonderful way to develop trust.

◆ I heard this song on the radio when I was a little girl. I can't recall the melody but I do remember the words, and I sang them to my babies.

> *Go to sleepy little baby,*
> *Go to sleepy little baby.*
> *When you wake,*
> *You'll patty, patty cake,*
> *And ride a shiny little pony.*

◆ Think of other lullabies. Sing or say them to your baby as you rock and sway and hold him close.

WHAT YOUR BABY WILL LEARN:
TRUST

Hold Me Close

◆ Rock the baby gently in your arms, back and forth in time to this rhyme. Say the words softly.

> *Hold me close, hold me close,*
> *Rock and rock and rock and rock.*
> *Hold me close, hold me close,*
> *Rock and rock my baby mine.*

◆ The rocking movement is familiar to the baby from being in the womb. This activity will bond you with the baby very quickly.

◆ WHAT YOUR BABY WILL LEARN:
RHYTHM

Listen to the Sounds

◆ Before nap time, sit the baby outside near a tree where she can watch the leaves move.

◆ Tie lightweight items to the branches. hear the sounds.

◆ Chimes, foil pie pans and necklaces make lovely sounds as the wind blows through them.

◆ Talk about the sounds to the baby. Use words like "soft," "high," "tinkling," and any others you think of. The sounds will be restful to the baby.

WHAT YOUR BABY WILL LEARN:
ABOUT SOUNDS

Baby's Bottle

◆ If your baby drinks from a bottle, you can help him experience different textures with this activity.

◆ Put a bottle cover on the bottle and let him feel it as he sucks.

◆ Use a sock instead of a commercial bottle cover.

◆ Experiment with different fabrics and see which ones your baby enjoys.

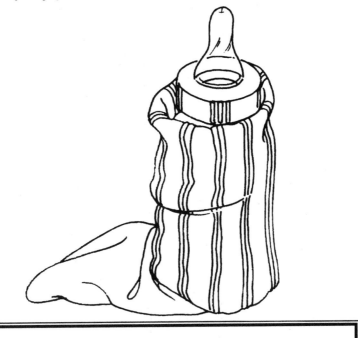

WHAT YOUR BABY WILL LEARN:
ABOUT TEXTURES

The Man in the Moon

◆ Hold your baby and look at the moon together.

◆ Say the word "moon" while pointing to the moon.

◆ Emphasize the word "moon" as you recite this rhyme to your baby.

> *The man in the moon*
> *Looked out of the moon,*
> *Looked out of the moon and said,*
> *"'Tis time for all of*
> *The children on earth*
> *To think about going to bed."*
> *Nighty night,*
> *Nighty night.*
> *Sleep tight,*
> *Sleep tight.*

◆ As you say, "nighty night" and "sleep tight," walk toward the bed with your baby.

◆ Repeat those words as you lay your baby down to sleep.

◆ WHAT YOUR BABY WILL LEARN:
LANGUAGE SKILLS

Back and Forth

◆ Rock your baby back and forth.

◆ Look straight into his eyes as you recite this rhyme.

Back and forth, I rock the baby,
Back and forth,
Back and forth.
Go to sleep my precious baby,
I will watch you all the night.

Back and forth, I rock the baby,
Back and forth,
Back and forth.
Pleasant dreams, my precious baby,
When you wake I'll be right here.

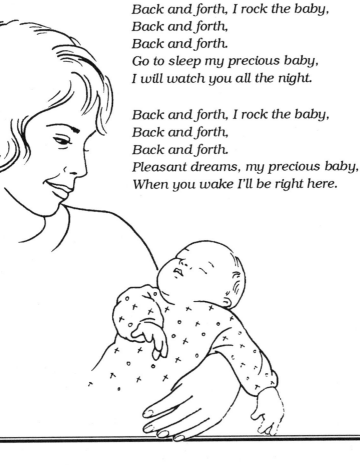

◆ WHAT YOUR BABY WILL LEARN:
BONDING

Let's Go to Bed

◆ Rock your baby gently to sleep as you recite this lovely rhyme.

Come let's go to bed, bed,
Come let's go to bed.
Rest your sleepy head, head,
Come let's go to bed.

Close your pretty eyes, eyes,
Close your pretty eyes.
Rest your sleepy head, head,
Close your pretty eyes.

◆ WHAT YOUR BABY WILL LEARN:
BONDING

Blow the Fire

◆ Your baby will find gentle puffs of breath on her body, accompanied by your soft voice, as you ready her for bed.

◆ As you change her diaper, recite:.

> *Little Sandy, blow the fire,*
> *(Use your baby's name)*
> *Puff, puff, puff.*
> *(Blow little puffs on the baby's tummy)*
> *Blow it very gently,*
> *(Blow gently)*
> *Blow it like the wind,*
> *(Blow with an "oooo" sound)*
> *Blow it for a kiss.*
> *(Kiss your baby's tummy)*

 WHAT YOUR BABY WILL LEARN:
BODY AWARENESS

Sleepy Time

◆ Recite this rhyme to your baby as you hold him close.

> *Sleepy time, little baby*
> *Sleepy time, little baby*
> *Sleepy time, little baby*
> *Here's a kiss for baby.*

◆ When you say, "sleepy time," sway back and forth or move around the room very slowly.

◆ Kiss the baby in a different place each time.

◆ Insert into the rhyme different parts of the body.

> *Sleepy time, little toesies....*
> *Sleepy time, little fingers....*
> *Sleepy time, little tummy....*

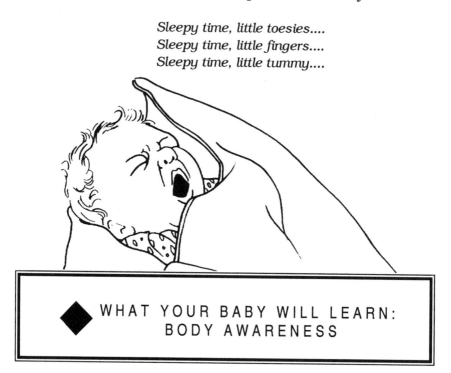

◆ WHAT YOUR BABY WILL LEARN:
BODY AWARENESS

Up and Down the Elevator

◆ Lift your baby up over your head and bring her down slowly to your face.

◆ When your faces touch, say, "I love you."

◆ Lift your baby into the air as you say, "Time to go up the elevator. Bye-bye."

◆ Bring your baby down again saying, "Time to come down the elevator," and kiss her on the cheek.

◆ After you have done this several times, hold the baby close and say, "Good night, sweet baby."

WHAT YOUR BABY WILL LEARN:
TRUST

Hush-a-Bye

◆ This is one of the loveliest lullabies that I know. It is American in origin, first sung in the South.

◆ If you do not know the melody, say the words in a sing-song fashion.

◆ Rock your baby while you sing. When I sang this to my babies, I changed "sleep" to "sleepy."

> *Hush-a-bye, don't you cry,*
> *Go to sleep, little baby.*
> *When you wake, you shall take*
> *All the pretty little horses.*
> *Blacks and bays, dapples and grays,*
> *Coach and six little horses.*
> *Hush-a-bye, don't you cry,*
> *Go to sleep, little baby.*

◆ Kiss your baby on the line, "Go to sleep, little baby."

WHAT YOUR BABY WILL LEARN: WARMTH AND TRUST

Stretch Up High

◆ This is a nice way to relax your baby before bedtime.

◆ Sit on the floor with your baby facing you. First recite the rhyme and act out the movement yourself. Do it a second time with the baby.

Stretch up high as tall as a house,
    (Stretch your hands up high in the air)
Curl up small, as small as a mouse.
    (Curl up small)
Now pretend you're very sleepy,
    (Yawn and put your hand over your mouth)
Let your whole body get sleepy.
    (Flop like a rag doll)
Flop your hands and flop your feet,
    (Flop hands and feet)
Close your eyes and go to sleep.
    (Pretend to sleep)

◆ **WHAT YOUR BABY WILL LEARN:**
RELAXATION

Baby Massage

◆ One of the most rewarding ways to bond with your baby is through massage.

◆ Like adults, babies collect tension in their bodies, which they often release by crying. Massage can release tension and help babies fall asleep.

◆ Rub some baby oil on your hands and slowly and gently massage your baby's chest and shoulders, arms and hands, hips, legs and feet.

◆ Continue massaging his back, face and head.

◆ As you massage the baby, sing a lullaby or say loving words.

WHAT YOUR BABY WILL LEARN: RELAXATION

Come Let's to Bed

◆ Rock your baby back and forth as you recite.

> *"Come let's to bed," says Sleepy Head.*
> *"Tarry a while," says Slow.*
> *"Put on the pan," says Greedy Nan.*
> *"We'll sup before we go."*

◆ Repeat the rhyme several times, talking more and more slowly each time.

◆ WHAT YOUR BABY WILL LEARN:
BONDING

The Wind Is Blowing

◆ Show your baby how the wind blows. Blow gently with your lips, and see if your baby can imitate you.

◆ Hold your baby close and recite:

> *The wind, the wind, is passing through,*
> *Rustling leaves, whispering to the trees.*
>
> *I'm the wet wind,*
> *I bring the summer rain,*
> *When I blow softly,*
> *I will whisper your name.*

◆ Put your baby's palm in front of your lips and blow gently as you whisper her name.

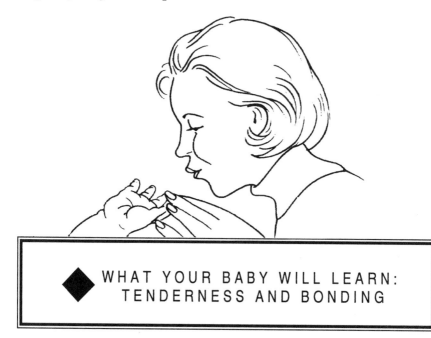

◆ **WHAT YOUR BABY WILL LEARN:**
TENDERNESS AND BONDING

Loo Loo Loo

◆ Singing songs that repeat the same syllable is a wonderful way to develop your child's language skills.

◆ Babies will imitate and practice a repeated sound.

◆ Lullabies traditionally included the sound "loo."

◆ Think of familiar lullabies, and as you rock your baby, sing the melody with the sound "loo."

◆ Lullabies you might know include: "Hush Little Baby," "Hush-A-Bye" and "brahm's Lullaby" ("Lullaby and Good Night"). Try to remember the songs sung to you as a child.

 WHAT YOUR BABY WILL LEARN:
LANGUAGE SKILLS

Hush, Little Baby

◆ Here are the words to a lovely traditional lullaby that you probably heard when you were a baby.

Hush little baby, don't say a word,
Papa's gonna buy you a mockingbird
If that mockingbird won't sing,
Papa's gonna buy you a diamond ring.
If that diamond ring turns brass,
Papa's gonna buy you a looking glass.
If that looking glass gets broke,
Papa's gonna buy you a billy goat.
If that billy goat won't pull,
Papa's gonna buy you a cart and bull.
If that cart and bull turn over,
Papa's gonna buy you a dog named Rover.
If that dog named Rover won't bark,
Papa's gonna buy you a horse and cart.
If that horse and cart fall down,
You'll still be the sweetest little baby in town.

◆ WHAT YOUR BABY WILL LEARN:
BONDING

9 - 12 MONTHS

Sleep Song

◆ Bedtime is a good time to sing to your baby.

◆ Sing this song to the tune of "Good Night, Ladies."

> *Good night, baby,*
>   *(insert your child's name)*
> *Good night, baby,*
> *Good night, baby,*
> *It's time to go to sleep.*
>
> *Sleep tight, baby,*
> *Sleep tight, baby,*
> *Sleep tight, baby,*
> *Time to close your eyes.*

◆ WHAT YOUR BABY WILL LEARN:
BONDING

Smile at Me

◆ Hold your baby and sing this song to her to the tune of "London Bridge Is Falling Down."

> *Baby, baby, smile at me,*
> *Smile at me,*
> *Smile at me,*
> *Baby, baby, smile at me,*
> *I love my baby.*

◆ When you say "I love my baby," kiss her gently on the cheek.

◆ WHAT YOUR BABY WILL LEARN:
BONDING

Wee Willie Winkie

◆ This popular and ageless nursery rhyme has charmed generations of children.

◆ Teach the rhyme to your child and encourage him to say the line "For now it's eight o'clock."

> *Wee Willie Winkie*
> *Runs through the town,*
> *Upstairs and downstairs*
> *In his nightgown.*
> *Rapping at the windows,*
> *Crying through the locks,*
> *"Are the children in their beds?*
> *For now it's eight o'clock."*

 WHAT YOUR BABY WILL LEARN:
LANGUAGE SKILLS

Niño Querido

◆ Rock and cuddle the baby in your arms, especially at bed-time.

◆ This is a lovely lullaby to sing to your baby just before bed. If you don't know the melody, make up your own. What's important are the words and feelings that the song conveys.

Niño querido, (neen-yoh kay-ree-tho)
Duermete ya (dwear-may-tay yah)
Que mientras tanto (kay myen-trahs
*   tahn-toh)*
Te canta mama. (tay kahn-tah mah-mah)
Niño querido, (neen-yoh kay-ree-tho)
Duermete ya. (dwear-may-tay yah)

Baby beloved, sleeping there
While Mother sings to her baby
*   fair.*
Baby beloved, sleeping there.

◆ **WHAT YOUR BABY WILL LEARN:**
LANGUAGE SKILLS

Newcastle Lullaby

◆ This is called a dandling song rather than a lullaby. A dandling song is sung while the baby eats and plays, before she is put in the cradle.

◆ Dandling songs can be spoken or sung. The sound of the language will be lovely for your child to hear.

◆ The words are Scottish in origin, and the song comes from Newcastle-upon-Tyne, near Scotland in northeast England's Northumberland County.

> *Sleep bonnie bairnie behind the castle*
> *By, by!*
> *By, by!*
> *Thou shalt have a golden apple*
> *By, by!*
> *By, by!*

◆ Rock your baby as you say the words. Hold her hands and gently move them each time you say, "by, by."

 WHAT YOUR BABY WILL LEARN: LANGUAGE SKILLS

Sleep Story

◆ Make up a story to tell your baby that uses his name.

◆ The story should describe things that your baby does during the day.

◆ Here is an example.

> Once upon a time there was a sweet little baby (your child's name). He played with his toys. Sometimes he would go outside to see the birds and the grass. At dinner time he drank his milk and ate his dinner.
>
> Every night, his mommy (or daddy) gave him a bath and lots of kisses. After his mommy (or daddy) laid him in his crib, he closed his eyes and went to sleep.

◆ Use your child's name in the story as often as possible.

◆ **WHAT YOUR BABY WILL LEARN:
LANGUAGE SKILLS**

I See the Moon

◆ Look outside with your child and talk about the moon and the stars.

◆ Tell your child that the moon and stars help people to fall asleep because they remind us that it is nighttime.

◆ Teach your child this poem about the moon and the stars.

> *I see the moon,*
> *And the moon sees me.*
> *God bless the moon,*
> *And God bless me.*
>
> *I see the stars,*
> *And the stars see me.*
> *God bless the stars,*
> *And God bless me.*

◆ Ask your child what else she sees and insert those things into the poem. For example:

> *I see mommy,*
> *And mommy sees me.*
> *God bless mommy,*
> *And God bless me.*

◆ **WHAT YOUR BABY WILL LEARN:**
A BEDTIME ROUTINE

Good Night, Sleep Tight

◆ This poem makes a wonderful bedtime routine. Your baby will become familiar with the pattern and look forward to it each evening.

◆ Show your baby the clock and say, "tick, tock."

◆ Show your baby the stars and say, "twinkle, twinkle."

◆ Recite the poem.

> *Good night, sweet baby,*
> *Good night, sweet one.*
> *The clock is ticking,*
> *And says we're done.*
> *Good night, sweet baby,*
> *Good night, my dear.*
> *The stars are twinkling,*
> *And sleep is near.*
>
> *Good night, sleep tight,*
> *Don't let the bedbugs bite.*

WHAT YOUR BABY WILL LEARN:
A BEDTIME ROUTINE

Index